FROM CLASSIC TO ROMANTIC:
PREMISES OF TASTE
IN
EIGHTEENTH-CENTURY ENGLAND

LONDON : GEOFFREY CUMBERLEGE
OXFORD UNIVERSITY PRESS

FROM CLASSIC TO ROMANTIC

PREMISES OF TASTE
IN
EIGHTEENTH–CENTURY ENGLAND

By

WALTER JACKSON BATE

1 9 4 6

HARVARD · UNIVERSITY · PRESS
CAMBRIDGE

To

ALFRED NORTH WHITEHEAD

PREFACE

The chapters of this book were presented as the Lowell Lectures, in Boston, in the spring of 1945. They treat a few aspects of a very large subject, the crucial transition which took place during the eighteenth century in European conceptions of the character, justification, and aim of art.

No similar transition has been more fundamental and pervasive. Many of the assumptions which had underlain ideas of art in classical antiquity and in the Renaissance were gradually supplanted at this time by more individualistic and psychological conceptions of art and taste; and these conceptions, under various names, have largely dominated our thinking about art to the present day. Perhaps more than any other single country, England introduced and encouraged this alteration of ideas, although England also ended by modifying and reabsorbing many of its effects into the main direction of English thought as a whole. The two series of conceptions immediately involved in this change have usually been put under the arbitrary headings of "classicism" and "romanticism." Both words are loose and inadequate, especially the term "romanticism." But continued use has given them such a number of connotations that they not only prove more convenient than others but even defy replacement.

The purpose of these lectures is to sketch some of the more significant outlines of this evolution or interchange of ideas: to describe the primary premises which underlay conceptions of taste or aesthetic judgment in English classicism and romanticism, and to connect the supplanting of the one by the other with the broader shift in European thought which it reflects. The general form of a lecture hardly lends itself, of course, to minute analysis;

it tends, on the contrary, to encourage an oversimplification of issues which are really complex. I hope that any such simplification here has not been more excessive than the general character of the subject justifies.

To the Trustee and Curator of the Lowell Institute, Messrs. Ralph Lowell and William Lawrence, I express my thanks for their invitation to present these lectures. Mr. John Bullitt will recognize the incorporation here of many different ideas which we have exchanged over some years, and I thank him also for helpful material which he generously placed at my disposal. Mr. A. H. Chroust and Mr. Richard Tansey have preserved me from making blunders when I have emerged into fields where I am far less competent than they. I am also obligated to the kindness of Professor Theodore Spencer for many helpful suggestions. No member of the Society of Fellows can fail to be aware of a great debt to Professor Alfred North Whitehead: as will be apparent to any of his readers, I owe much to his penetrating insights into the intellectual issues of both the eighteenth century and other periods; and I am obligated generally to his ready good sense and suggestive counsel. To the Society of Fellows as a whole I wish to express my gratitude for the opportunity to investigate further the subjects which these lectures attempt to summarize. Finally, my special thanks are due to Professors George Sherburn, Harry Levin, and Douglas Bush for their patient interest and salutary advice.

CONTENTS

CHAPTER I.

THE CLASSIC AND NEO–CLASSIC PREMISES

Conceptions of the nature and purpose of art closely parallel man's conceptions of himself and of his destiny. For art, in one of its primary functions, is the interpreter of values, and aesthetic criticism, when it rises above mere technical analysis, attempts to grasp and estimate these values in order to judge the worth of the interpretation. The period which is often called the European Enlightenment — a period which extends roughly from the middle of the seventeenth century through the close of the eighteenth — is in this sense the transitional meeting-ground between two dominant epochs of modern thinking.

The earlier portion of the Enlightenment marks the final subsiding of the European Renaissance: it comprises the consolidation and in some respects the extreme development of the values it inherited. Concluding as it did a Renaissance of extraordinary intellectual activity, it possessed ready at hand a body of conceptions which had been widely urged in philosophical and scientific writing and brilliantly exemplified in all the arts. Much of its inheritance consisted of a collective system of values to which— because of the lack of any more specific or generally accepted term — the broad and chameleon-like word "humanism" has often been applied. The word may be easily disputed. But whatever term we apply to it, this general outlook or system of values is one which largely permeated classical thought, and also received some qualification and re-direction by Christian elements in the later Middle Ages and the Renaissance. Though indefinite and even vague in a few of its exterior ramifications, it was always unified in its funda-

mental purpose and approach: it viewed man's intellectual and moral
nature as ideally the same, and it assumed as its goal the evolution
of the total man in accordance with that view. It especially emphasized man's ethical "reason" as his own distinctive nature, and as
the means of gaining insight into the ideal and of comprehending
the standard or end which this ideal comprises. Humanism, as it is
used in this special sense, is almost another word for classicism
itself. Similarly, the codification of some of the means and premises
which Renaissance humanism postulated for the attainment or
portrayal of this standard, the carrying to an extreme conclusion
of others, and the inevitable counteractions to which this codification gave rise, may, in a general sense, be said to comprise neo-
classicism as an historical phenomenon. And within these codifica-
tions and reactions the various neo-classic conceptions of taste
largely reside.

I

On a journey through France with the Thrales, Dr. Johnson,
while the scenery was being admired, impatiently retorted: "A
blade of grass is always a blade of grass, whether in one country
or another. . . . Men and women are my subjects of inquiry; let
us see how these differ from those we have left behind." The statement is reminiscent of that made by Socrates to Phaedrus, as the
two reclined on the bank of the Ilyssus: "I am a lover of knowledge; and the men who dwell in the city are my teachers, and
not the trees or the country." Such sentiments would have elicited
at least some agreement from any classicist, even a less sternly
ethical one than was Socrates or Johnson. The absence or the
depreciation of the landscape in Greek and Roman art is no historical accident: whether the classical artist sought to portray physical
or moral beauty, his attention was directed to its existence and its
ideal potentiality in the human being. Similarly, to Michelangelo
and Raphael, and to the enormous group of artists which pivots
about them, the landscape was of merely complementary interest.

As late as 1719 the Abbé du Bos could write, with reasonable representativeness:

The finest landskip, were it even Titian's or Caraccio's, does not affect us. . . . The most knowing painters have been so thoroughly convinced of this truth, that it is rare to find any *mere* landskips of theirs without an intermixture of figures. They have therefore thought proper to people them, as it were, by introducing into their pieces a subject composed of several personages, whereof the action might be capable of moving, and consequently of engaging us.[1]

The classical direction of art to human actions and potentialities mirrors the traditional humanistic stress upon moral knowledge and cultivation rather than upon the scientific investigation of the external world. The classical moralist, without being narrowly dogmatic, might still dissent from the view of a recent scientist who took issue with Terence's statement, *Homo sum, humani nil a me alienum puto* — "I am a man, and consider nothing that is human to be foreign to me" — and who thought it should be altered to read: "I am a space-time event, and I deem nothing that is a space-time event to be foreign to me." "Our business here," said Locke, humanistic even in his empiricism, "is not to know all things, but those which concern our conduct." A fair number of early eighteenth-century satires, of which that in *Gulliver's Travels* on the Academy of Lagado is the preëminent example, rest upon this conviction. The activities with which the Academy was occupied — extracting sunbeams out of cucumbers, condensing air into a tangible substance, making gunpowder from ice, attempting to plot the date of the sun's eventual extinction — are instanced by Swift to signify an amoral tendency to be "curious and conceited in matters where we have least concern, and for which we are least adapted either by study or nature." Gulliver's Houyhnhnm master, in the fourth voyage, found it strange that "a creature pretending to *Reason*" should devote himself much to "natural philosophy";

[1] *Critical Reflections on Poetry, Painting, and Music* (tr. Thomas Nugent, 1748), I, 44.

and he concluded that, if mankind were not destroyed through the growing horror of war, such an indiscriminate devotion would only "multiply our original wants," and then lead us "to spend our whole lives in vain endeavours to supply them by our own inventions."

To Dr. Johnson, again, only the study of man's ideals and conduct deserves to be called "intercourse with intellectual nature":

> The knowledge of external nature, and the sciences which that knowledge requires or includes, are not the great or frequent business of the human mind. Whether we provide for action or conversation, . . . the first requisite is the religious and moral knowledge of right and wrong; the next is an acquaintance with the history of mankind, and with those examples which may be said to embody truth, and prove by events the reasonableness of opinions. . . . We are perpetually moralists, but we are geometricians only by chance. Our intercourse with intellectual nature is necessary; our speculations upon matter are voluntary, and at leisure.[2]

Consequently, as Johnson elsewhere stated, "He who thinks reasonably must think morally." To the classicist, indeed, any rational evaluation of the beautiful was, in the widest implication of the word, a moral one, which simultaneously transcended and gauged or controlled the worth of strictly aesthetic feelings or reactions; nor would the classicist have taken very seriously Poe's attack on those who attempt "to reconcile the obstinate oils and waters of Poetry and Truth."

With such a direction and aim assumed for art, the classical and Renaissance conception of the poet as a teacher of moral excellence was a logical conclusion. "For what ought we to admire the poet?" asked Aristophanes; and his answer was "because the poet makes better men." The good can be conceived and then taught only by the good; and the insistence of Cicero, Quintilian, and others that the orator must first of all be a good man was repeatedly applied to the poet in Renaissance and eighteenth-century criticism. Again,

[2] *Life of Milton, Works* (1820), IX, 91.

since his concern is man, the poet must be versed in the customs
and manners of men, not as they are found under local and
temporary conditions, but as they mirror the immutable principles
and aspirations of human beings throughout history. The constancy
of the basic working of human nature is stressed in most early
eighteenth-century writing. A characteristic contention is an article
in the *British Magazine* (1760) which has as its subject the "similitude of genius" in Horace, Boileau, and Pope as indicative of "that
ingenious observation of Plutarch, that Nature delights in repro-
ducing the same characters." Or, similarly, Richard Hurd, in his
"Discourse on Poetical Imitation," defends apparent imitation of
earlier works on the basis that both the passions and manners are
"constant in their effects," and successive writers must necessarily
deal with much the same situations.

The profit gained from history is ethical in that it furnishes aid
in estimating what is general and what is merely accidental.
"History's chief use," said Hume, "is only to discover the constant
and universal principles of human nature." In the *Tour to the
Hebrides,* Boswell records Monboddo as stating: "The history of
manners is the most valuable. I never set a high value on any other
history":

JOHNSON. "Nor I; and therefore I esteem biography, as giving us what
comes near to ourselves. . . ." BOSWELL. "But in the course of general
history, we find manners. In wars, we see the dispositions of people, their
degrees of humanity, and other particulars." JOHNSON. "Yes; but then
you must take all the facts to get this, and it is but a little you get."
MONBODDO. "And it is that little which makes history valuable." [8]

The long and hearty duration of classical antiquity's experience
with society, and the brilliant interpretation which it evolved, made
both the history of its experience and the study of its verdicts of
primary value to the artist's comprehension of man's ideal and
general nature; and the authority of antiquity, as a consequence,

[8] (Edd. Pottle and Bennett, 1936), p. 55.

was continually upheld. John Dennis censured Pope's failure to state more precisely from what the ideal of man's nature is to be taken; and he added that Horace had not merely told his readers that the principal source of good writing is moral learning, but had "pointed to the very Books where they might find that moral Philosophy" — that is, the works of Plato.

The prevalence of didactic art in the late seventeenth and early eighteenth centuries, and the frequent employment in criticism of purely didactic values, are a somewhat extreme development of this premise. Aristotle had stated that the subject of poetry, though necessarily ethical in purpose, was less the exposition of moral theory than the revelation of "the manners of men"; and Renaissance critics, as in Scaliger's admonition that "the poet teaches character through *actions*," generally reiterated this distinction. Joseph Trapp, lecturing at Oxford early in the eighteenth century, stressed the ethical end of poetry as illustrative and not as didactically explanatory; and a similar emphasis is not uncommon in other English critics of the day. But in practice, and somewhat in precept, the late seventeenth century increasingly inclined towards the didactic direction which Roman poetry, proceeding from an ethical standpoint, had also taken. The unhesitating adoption of the verse-essay by Boileau, Pope, and a plentiful number of other writers is symptomatic of the evolution; and the same may be said to some extent of the pronounced contemporary rise of verse-satire, which, Dryden maintained, "is of the nature of moral philosophy, as being instructive." The famous attack on the *Immorality and Profaneness of the English Stage* (1698) by Jeremy Collier, who regarded criticism as irresponsible and even harmful if it did not put into practice the moral considerations it extolled, was only a vigorous application of the precepts of Boileau, Rapin, Dacier, and indeed the bulk of Renaissance and eighteenth-century critics. Scaliger, although Aristotle had thought differently, had emphasized the necessity of portraying, in the drama, the reward of virtue and the punishment of vice; D'Aubignac and others considered this "the most indispensable rule of dramatic poetry"; and the occasional critical premium throughout the eighteenth century on "poetic justice" — which was given its name by Thomas Rymer, and which had as many opponents as it had adherents — exemplifies an extreme development and subsequent petrification of the broad humanistic conception of the poet's ethical function.

II

Arising from the classical assumption that man's reason and his moral nature are one is the belief that character can be justly formed and guided only by a genuine insight into the universal, and by the rational grasp of the decorum, measure, and standard which characterize the ideal. The portrayal of the universal in art — the exhibition, in other words, of the general in the particular, of the one in the many — can achieve permanent success only if the particulars employed are reasonably common to the experience of cultivated mankind throughout successive generations. Indeed, the most pervasive single tendency of almost all classicism may be defined, as Mr. Santayana has said, by the phrase "the idealization of the familiar." The achievement of this goal may utilize various means; but they are in all cases related directly to man, and are based upon man's common intellectual, aesthetic, and moral experience and interest. The representation of familiar examples of character; the embodiment of the ideal potentialities of the human figure, as in classical and Renaissance sculpture; the illustration of the working of primary and elementary feelings and passions, divorced from situations peculiar only to a specific locality or time; the delineation of the progress and objective significance of those climactic occurrences of destiny, especially death, which are common to all, and of the manner in which human reactions to such occurrences most fully and nobly reveal themselves; and, above all, the expression in such types, postures, attitudes, exertions, or passions, of those laws and indeed heroic ideals which are manifested and held by the most exemplary in all ages and places: —

the employment, depiction, and idealization of these form the province and purpose of classical art.

A corollary of this dedication to the elementary and primary had always been, in classical thought, an emphasis on clarity of expression. To the ancient rhetoricians, such as Cicero and Quintilian, one of the first requisites of art had been lucidity and immediacy of communication. And the widespread preoccupation of Restoration and early eighteenth-century British critics with simplicity of style, the attacks on complicated metaphor by such writers as Thomas Sprat, John Eachard, and Lord Lansdowne, the stress on the employment of an idiom and of stylistic devices which, from long sanction and use, had become intimately and prevalently known, the growing disfavor with which "metaphysical" verse was viewed, the common attitude towards poetry as a branch of rhetoric, the painstaking attempt by later critics to outline concretely the means by which clarity of diction, metaphor, and sentence-structure might be attained — often accompanied by appeal to the authority of classical rhetoricians — such tendencies, though they reveal other intentions as well, are a neo-classic reassertion of the importance of the familiar as far as stylistic values are concerned.

"*Truth* in poetry," said Hurd, paraphrasing Horace, "means such an expression as conforms to the general nature of things: *falsehood,* that which, however suitable to the particular instance in view, doth yet not correspond to such *general nature.*" And the classical aesthetic values of unity, simplicity, and the natural and harmonious adaptation of parts to the whole are founded upon a confidence in the truth and grandeur of ordered generality. They may be said to stand opposed, for example, to the romantic cherishing of the surprise in variety, the wonder and mystery in contemplating the strange and occasionally the grotesque, which attend upon an indiscriminate amusement and transitory delight in the particular.

This emphasis on the stripping of all that is extraneous and accidental in the portrayal of the familiar is not to be confused, of course, with the intention of "naturalism." To the classicist, "naturalism," especially in its more extreme form, could be only a partial view of phenomena. Its essentially empirical standpoint, that is, would display a disregard of those fundamental realities which only the ideal can signify and declare; and, to take but one instance, the classicist postulated as a general rule that the writing of tragedy could have little success without a judicious selection of the characters portrayed. The feelings and thoughts of the character can be participated in and can be said to have significance only in proportion as the character himself is capable of feeling and thinking. Oedipus, Antigone, Prometheus, and Lear are tragic characters; Wordsworth's Betty Foy, "the idiot mother of the idiot boy," or Harry Gill, who is continually cold and whose "teeth chatter, chatter still," are hapless enough beings, but they have hardly the significance of Hamlet. "How shall our attention," said the Abbé du Bos, "be engaged by a picture representing a peasant driving a couple of beasts along the highway?" Such a picture "may possibly amuse us some few moments, and may even draw from us an applause of the artist's abilities in imitating, but can never raise any emotion or concern." Painters of genuine insight do not picture

a man going along the highroad, or . . . a woman carrying fruit to market; they commonly present us with figures that *think*, in order to make us think; they paint men hurried with passions, to the end that ours may also be raised, and our attention fixed by this very agitation.[4]

The naturalistic writer, it is true, attempts to approach the norm, and to discard the adventitious; but at least the more extreme naturalist may be said, in a sense, to assume the lowest as the norm, and to view whatever is better as an unexpected if happy gain or as helpful to "progress"; while the classicist conceives the highest as the norm, and regards whatever falls below, not as "natural," but as corruption. The difference resides in the interpretation of

[4] *Reflections*, I, 42, 44–45.

"nature." To the naturalist, nature is inevitably what he empirically judges as reality, in which any human idealization discovered is not inherent or actual but either something superimposed, something simply displayed as a psychological reaction of human beings under given circumstances, or at best something useful or desirable for the social, scientific, and humanitarian betterment of mankind. The various shades of meaning in the use of the word "nature" in English neo-classic thought have been sufficiently traced, especially by Mr. Lovejoy, and need not be recapitulated here. It is sufficient to state that in general the classical conception of nature, from the Greeks to almost the middle of the eighteenth century, is that central idea and form which the particular struggles to attain; and when Aristotle defined poetry as an "imitation of nature," he did not mean the indiscriminate copying of any individual, but rather the selective imitation of what is general and representative in man. Dennis condemned Pope for not defining "nature" in as unmistakably plain detail as Horace, who

makes it as clear as the Sun, what it is to follow Nature in giving us a draught of human Life, and of the manners of Men, and that is, not to draw after particular Men, who are but Copies and imperfect Copies of the great universal Pattern; but to consult that innate Original, and that universal Idea, which the Creator has fix'd in the minds of ev'ry reasonable Creature.[5]

"What is natural," said Grotius, "we must judge by those in whom nature is *least* corrupt"; and those who serve as concrete if not wholly ideal standards for the natural are "those who are most civilized." The conception of "nature" as the ultimate standard, as the essential meaning and final aim of life, underlies the classical conviction that the end of art is the revelation to man and the rational, ethical inculcation in him of that ideal perfection of which, in a degree varying according to his own character, he as a particular is only a faulty image.

[5] *Reflections upon a Late Rhapsody Called an Essay upon Criticism* (1711), p. 31.

III

In its devotion to the rationally conceived ideal, classicism is opposed not only to the naturalistic but to any other conception of art which can be designated as personal or local — to the conception of art, in other words, as sheer emotional experience for its own sake, as intellectual amusement, or as propaganda. It views the mere stimulation of emotional excitement and the unschooled liberation of impulses as at best a temporary narcotic, the awakening from which inevitably brings in its train — as some later aspects of European romanticism were perhaps to illustrate — a dichotomy of mind and feeling, and a dissatisfaction based not so much on intellectual conviction and criticism as on mere insecurity of feeling.

From the universal character of its ethical standpoint, classicism draws a marked distinction between centrality and diversity, between man's unified rational grasp of his ideal nature, and his peripheral and independent development, as a particular, of the impulses and reactions which comprise what is occasionally called his personality. Indeed, classicism assumes that only through the former can genuine individual fulfillment be found. For it regards man's feelings as by themselves helpless, blind, and eminently susceptible to dictation of some sort. They are not, that is, free to determine themselves, but are inevitably led by something else: they are subject to whatever is in closest or most vital proximity to them — whether it be a rationally determined end which is vividly and firmly held in the mind, or whether, if this end be lacking, it be merely whatever external environment chance may offer. It is in this respect that Dr. Johnson could state, with complete practicality: "Whatever withdraws us from the power of our senses, whatever makes the past, the distant, or the future predominate over the present, advances us in the dignity of thinking beings." True individual freedom accrues in the channeling of man's responses towards an end which reason conceives to transcend the local and temporary; its opposite exists when such a formative and determining conception is lacking, and habit is established through chance, fashion, local custom, or individual caprice.

Classicism does not subscribe, therefore, to the belief that man's feelings and responses are themselves inherently good — a belief which was to underlie at least some romantic assumptions towards the close of the eighteenth century. And just as art itself is inadequate when it is conditioned largely by the customs and opinions of a transitory society, or when its primary purpose is to serve either as an emotional narcotic or as an esoteric exercise of ingenuity; similarly, in the role of the artist as propagandist, as an indulger in subjective sensibility, or as the mere craftsman, there is much that fails to attain and indeed obstruct what, in the classical sense, a man should be.

To rest a determination of values upon the feelings, the floating inclinations, or the varying empirically-held opinions of particular individuality is to rest it upon the most fluid of foundations. For the abandonment of the centrally ideal by empirical relativism not only results in a conflict of predilections from man to man, but, as Irving Babbitt so frequently insisted, in conflict and change within even the same man. Its probable consequence, of which European art and thought of the past century contain frequent instances, may be typified by D. H. Lawrence's rather confused assertion: "I am many men. . . . Who are you? How many selves have you? And which of these selves do you want to be?"; and the classicist might question whether an even more ultimate conclusion was not exemplified in a recent poem which begins with the declaration "I am four monkeys," and concludes with the question "How many monkeys are you?" Against the fluidity and relativism of either personal or else local and fashionable predilection, classicism places universal "nature" as that centripetal and "just standard" which, said Pope, is "at once the source, and end, and test of art," and which also comprises, in its broad ethical character, "the source, and end, and test" of all that may be called the ideal of man.

"Besides the purging of the passions," said Thomas Rymer, poetry infuses order and justness of comprehension into the mind simply by its reflection, in the form and outline of its own structure, of "that constant order, that harmony and beauty of Providence." [6] For the very nature of the universal, in its transcendence and control over the accidental and specific, exemplifies order and harmony; and the living exhibition of order and the persuasive infiltration of it into man's moral and mental character are both a vital aspect of the means by which art simultaneously "delights and teaches," and also an end for which it performs these functions. It is ethical in furnishing both the process and the aim.

With the same assumption, the notable classical discussions, such as that in Plato's *Republic*, of the fundamental importance of music in the ethical inculcation of order, measure, and harmony, are occasionally repeated and applied with historical pertinence in neo-classic criticism. Characteristic is a book by the opponent of Shaftesbury, John Brown, one of the purposes of which is to illustrate that, in past cultures, "As every change of Manners influenced their Music, so by a reciprocal Action, every Considerable Change of Music influenced their Manners." When music had attained in Greece a sufficiently high development in order and universality of form, it was rightly esteemed, said Brown, as

a *necessary Accomplishment:* And an Ignorance of this Art was regarded as a capital Defect. Of this we have an Instance, even in Themistocles himself, who was upbraided with his Ignorance in Music. The whole Country of *Cynaethe* laboured under a parallel Approach: And all the enormous *Crimes* committed there, were attributed by the neighbouring States to the *Neglect* of *Music.* — What wonder? For according to the Delineation here given of ancient Greek Music, their ignorance implied a general Deficiency in the three great articles of a social Education, *Religion, Morals,* and *Polity.*[7]

---

[6] *The Tragedies of the Last Age, Considered and Examined by the Practice of the Ancients and by the Common Sense of All Ages* (1678), p. 140.

[7] *Dissertation on the Rise, Union, and Power, the Progressions, Separations, and Corruptions of Poetry and Music* (1763), pp. 126–127.

The classical doctrine of exemplifying order in art often finds a humanistically Christian expression in eighteenth-century criticism as it had even more frequently in the Renaissance. "The great Design of Arts," Dennis maintained, "is to restore the Decays that happen'd to human Nature by the Fall, by restoring Order"; and "if the end of Poetry," he added, "be to instruct and reform the World, that is, to bring Mankind from Irregularity, Extravagance, and Confusion, to Rule and Order, how this should be done by a thing that is in itself irregular and extravagant, is difficult to be conceiv'd." [8] Poetry, as Aristotle had pointed out, possesses a more general truth than does history, and presents, in its selection and form, a model or imitation of more valid pertinence. And the representation of order being an aesthetic end, it must, as Charles Gildon said, "have certain Means of attaining that End, which are the *Rules* of *Art*."

IV

The primary rule may perhaps be defined as *decorum*. In Aristotelian and indeed most classical use of the term, decorum consists in the simultaneous "preservation and ennobling of the type" — in a faithful adherence to a probability of manners and language in the dramatic character and, at the same time, in a deepening of the import of this probability by disclosing its connection, not merely with temporary or social law, but with that which reason conceives as universal and ideal. Decorum, especially in neo-classic thought, was occasionally developed to certain conclusions and conventions which were perhaps as contradictory to the general rule of decorum as any other excess would be. Thus, the insistence on the unity and probability of a character's actions found a somewhat extreme ramification in the theory of the "ruling passion," which was perhaps more widespread in neo-classic precept, if not practice, than in the Renaissance. Yet the theory of the "ruling passion" was hardly universal; and the moderate issue which Dryden took with it was by no means unique:

[8] *Grounds of Criticism in Poetry* (1704), chap. ii.

A character, or that which distinguishes one man from all others, cannot be supposed to consist of one particular virtue, or vice, or passion only; but 'tis a composition of qualities which are not contrary to one another in the same person; thus, the same man may be liberal and valiant, but not liberal and covetous . . . yet it is still to be observed, that the virtue, vice, or passion, ought to be shown in every man, as predominant over all the rest.[9]

A similar rather confined application of the rule of decorum was frequently made in respect to rank or condition: even Dryden, for example, states that "when a poet has given the dignity of a king to one of his persons, in all his actions and speeches that person must discover majesty, magnanimity, and jealousy of power, because these are suitable to the general manners of a king"; and similar assertions are a commonplace throughout eighteenth-century European criticism. Still, such an application — though rather absurd, as Johnson pointed out, when measured against a broader interpretation of decorum — cannot appear as an extreme aberration when one recalls that many of the social distinctions of classical and Renaissance life had, in a sense, something of an intellectual justification in that underlying conception of "degree" and order which the aesthetic principles of classicism and neo-classicism also reflect.

The rule and order of decorum are of special importance in the total formation and unraveling of the outline or plot of action in dramatic or epic poetry. "The manners, in a poem," said Dryden, "are understood to be those inclinations, whether natural or acquired, which move and carry us to actions, good, bad, or indifferent . . . ; or which incline the persons to such or such actions." If several inclinations or actions, for example, have a common source in their past, they are immanent in that past; and again, since that source is perpetuated, as it were, in the subsequent inclinations or actions to which it gives rise, those resulting phenomena have a degree of immanence in each other.

With its goal of rendering vital the probability and ideal mean-

[9] *Preface to Troilus and Cressida, Essays* (ed. Ker, 1926), I, 215.

ing which compose decorum, art seeks to declare the unity of this immanence; it attempts, in other words, to descry and exhibit the order and law disclosed in the interweaving of past, present, and future, of event and inclination, of action and ideal. It was earlier stated that, in the classical conception, the very nature of unity or order presupposes for its delineation an ordered approach, an approach, in fact, which necessitates *rule*. "If the rules be well considered," Dryden quotes from Rapin, "we shall find them to be made only to reduce Nature into method, to trace her step by step, and not to suffer the least mark to escape us: 'tis only by these, that probability . . . is maintained, which is the soul of poetry." [10] The interplay of action, motive, and event in the *Iliad*, as might be expected, is summarized and extolled with special frequency, and usually with the purpose of illustrating, as Gildon says, that "this productive Chain of Incidents, in the *Iliad*, could not be formed without admirable Art and Design; and consequently, by such Rules as no Man since has ever been able to alter for the better." The often unfavorable attitude in neo-classic criticism towards many of the more exuberant romances of the Renaissance was largely conditioned by the importance attributed to a simple but closely interwoven unity of action. The ordered construction of the *Iliad*, for example, presents a strong contrast with the lack of it in such a poem as Spenser's *Faerie Queene*, which D'Avenant regarded as a dream "such as Poets and Painters, by being over-studious, may have in the beginning of Feavers," and which even neo-classic admirers of Spenser, like John Hughes, thought hopelessly "distracting" in its "want of Unity."

Among the dramatic rules formulated as subordinate and contributory to the broad governing rule of decorum, the most preëminent, and later the most controversial, were the famous "unities." It is characteristic of the empiricism which he accelerated, and which a century later gave support to the frequent romantic concern with the individual particular, that Thomas

[10] *Preface to Troilus and Cressida, Essays,* I, 213.

Hobbes should have considered the design and plot of a poem as less important than the language; and it is equally characteristic that Dryden should have censured him for doing so:

Mr. Hobbes, in the preface to his own bald translation of the *Iliad* (studying poetry as he did mathematics, when it was too late) . . . begins the praise of Homer where he should have ended it. He tells us that the first beauty of an epic poem consists in diction; that is, in the choice of words, and harmony of numbers. Now the words are the colouring of the work, which, in the order of nature, is last to be considered. The design, the disposition, manners, and the thoughts, are all before it.[11]

It is the *"Fable* or *Plot,"* states Rymer, "which all conclude to be the *Soul* of a *Tragedy;* which, with the *Ancients,* is always found to be a *reasonable Soul;* but *with us,* for the most part, a *brutish.* . . ."[12] "The most beautiful colors laid on without proportion," Aristotle had said, "will not give as much pleasure as the chalk outline of a portrait." The neo-classic doctrine of the "unities," which are frequently compared with "proportion" in painting, constitutes a rather exaggerated offshoot and codification of the classical emphasis on the order and probability of interrelation in the total structure of plot or outline.

Aristotle had mentioned the importance of a "unity of action" — a coherence and order, as a single whole, of events and conclusion. As for the unities of "place" and of "time," he said nothing at all about the former; and, about the latter, he merely observed that, in Greek poetry, the length of time elapsing in the action of dramatic tragedy differs from that of the epic: "For tragedy endeavors, as far as possible, to confine itself to a single revolution of the sun, or but slightly to exceed this limit; whereas the action of the epic has no limit of time." Aristotle's tentative statement about the customary practice of Greek tragedy was hardened into a rule in the first half of the sixteenth century by the Italian critic Giraldi Cintio:

[11] Preface to the *Fables, Essays,* II, 252.
[12] *Tragedies of the Last Age,* p. 4.

within another two or three generations, the restriction to a single day of the time of action in the drama had become a prevalent rule of decorum; and some critics, like Minturno, basing their deduction on the time covered in the *Iliad* and the *Aeneid*, attempted to restrict the action of the epic to a year.

Similarly, in the latter half of the sixteenth century, another Italian, Castelvetro, formulated the rule of the "unity of place" on the ground that, since its action takes place before our eyes, the drama would lose all verisimilitude, all probability, if a change of place were made in the course of it. Castelvetro became so enamored of the unities of time and place, and perhaps also of the prospect of the ingenuity which would be necessary to satisfy them, that he considered the one unity upon which Aristotle had insisted — the unity of action — as quite secondary, and as merely a convenient means of helping to fulfill the requirements of the other two! Within a hundred years after Castelvetro, the unity of place, like that of time, had achieved as much vogue and as much ingenuity of application as even he could have desired. But by the middle of the eighteenth century, these two unities were taken with less seriousness than is sometimes supposed; and Johnson was not alone in regarding them as giving "more trouble to the poet, than pleasure to the auditor," and in considering a drama that observed them "as an elaborate curiosity, as the product of superfluous and ostentatious art, by which is shewn rather, what is possible, than what is necessary."

v

It is the inherent order and proportion of the whole which comprises, in Pope's words, "the naked nature, and the living grace":

> 'Tis not the lip, or eye, we beauty call,
> But the joint force and full result of all.

Aristotle's emphasis on plot rather than on the portrayal of particular characters — his insistence, in other words, that man be revealed through the instrumentality of ordered actions rather than that events be shown through the medium of the feelings and identities of particular men — may be said to illustrate the classical conviction that poetry should seek less to arouse and give voice to the personal associations and feelings of the observer than to guide them, and to impose upon them a finished ideal. The representation of the human being in classical sculpture or painting has a similar end: it does not, by the portrayal of individual "expression" in its model, seek to evoke images from past experiences and thus appeal to the affections and associations of the beholder, but rather, by an imitation of the ideal, to form and control those affections and associations. Such a purpose is ethical in the very broadest sense of the word: for the classical attempt to embody, in plot, design, rhythm, or visual proportion, an "imitation" of the fundamental order and decorum of the universal is not to be viewed as "abstraction" but rather as "integration" and completion; it aspires to present an ideal end and a finished totality which the distinctive "expression" of the model, as a particular, cannot give.

Individual portraiture in painting or sculpture, for example, necessarily diverts art from the whole to only a specific performance and to an incomplete disclosure of one's personal identity. Classical sculpture, on the other hand, does not essay very often the piecemeal and miscellaneous expression of isolated actions, or of such single facets of individual character as would necessarily result from the representation of a given act, position, or facial feature. It endeavors, rather, to picture, in the light of an ideal, the total capacity of the human figure, and to endow it with that completeness which would have originally been formed and determined only by multifarious and rounded activities. It seeks to offer a concluded and integrated synthesis of all ideal human aspects, which, since they cannot be articulated in single performances without the exclusion of some of them and the loss of completeness and unison, are presented, as it were, potentially rather than kinetically, and as in perpetual readiness rather than in active execution.

Xenophon records Socrates as saying that "It is the business of the sculptor to represent in bodily form the energies of the spirit." The spirit, the ideal, is neither a means nor a reaction: it is an end, a fruition. It signifies the *ethos* or "character" — which is eternal and changeless — rather than the *pathos* or "feeling," which is passing and in flux. And from the revelation of the potentialities of this fruition, of this changeless *ethos,* and from the subduing and disciplining of these potentialities to the consonance and decorum of the ideal, arise the inherent finality, the repose and serenity, which are the properties of classical sculpture, architecture, and writing. "We are lovers of beauty," said Pericles of the Athenians, but of beauty "in its *frugal* forms." Similarly, music deserves to be specified as integrated rather than abstract when it becomes classical: when, disregarding appeal to subjective mood or transitory fashion, it weaves a disciplined structure from simple chords and melodies, and, combining with freedom and spontaneity a rational decorum of selection and design, renders audible and definite the potentialities of that proportion and form which alone may be said to constitute the universal in music.

Beneath the classical conception of the ideal and of the essential order, rule, and harmony which characterize it, is, of course, a general conviction in the absoluteness of divine law. The humanistic watchword for the knowledge of this law, as Mr. Bush's lectures on humanism have shown,[13] is *sapientia,* which Cicero defined as the knowledge of "the bonds of union between divinity and man and the relations of man to man." It had been the invaluable contribution of the Greek Sophists to illustrate that the material world, without exception, is characterized by continual flux; and as eighteenth and nineteenth-century empiricism itself, pursuing its logical evolution, was at length to conclude, the forces which dominate or issue from the material world are equally changing. To the "humanist," therefore, — in the sense in which the word has been used in this chapter — the law to which man by his intrinsic nature

[13] *The Renaissance and English Humanism* (Toronto: 1939), chap. ii.

is subjected is not to be confused with the forces, intelligible or un-intelligible, which appear to operate in the phenomenal and animal world, or with such compulsions or necessities as appear to play upon the individual man when he is considered as an atom in social dynamics. Indeed, the humanistic contention is that man possesses an end of his own; that his distinctive privilege consists in his ability to conceive the character of this ideal end; and that for man to be "natural" does not mean for him to live in accordance with what he judges the phenomenal world to be — as both romantic primi-tivism and empirical science were, in their varying ways, to encour-age him to do — but rather to manifest the absolute and centrally unified "nature," the joint ethical and rational fruition, which is at once his obligation and prerogative to fulfill. For the grasping of the nature of this ideal, and for comprehending its ethical import, Renaissance humanistic thought, in the main, had assumed three means, the complete employment of any one of which neces-sarily involved the employment of the others.

The philosophical conception of the universal was given its original formulation, of course, by Plato; and from the specific issues raised by him, almost all the extensions, re-applications, and contradictions of the theory of universals take their distinctive direction. The history of European philosophy, Mr. Whitehead has said, is "a series of footnotes to Plato." Certainly, since the delineation of most arguments proving the existence and character of the ideal is essentially a recapitulation of the bulk of classical thought, humanistic writers of the Renaissance continually empha-sized the importance of classical authority. Even in such a figure as Montaigne, "the vagabondage and egotism," as one critic has said, "are more or less superficial. What we find under the surface is a fairly firm conviction, based on the Greek, and especially the Latin, classics, as to what the true man should be." Again, the humanistic conception of what comprises "natural law" — the law, order, and character, that is to say, of the universal — was strongly inter-woven with Christian elements: in this sense, it continues, of course, a widespread tendency of medieval thought; and the complete indebtedness of Grotius to Aquinas and the Spanish Thomists, as Mr. Chroust has shown, is an outstanding example.

Lastly, and like classicism itself, Renaissance humanism placed its confidence in that faculty which alone distinguishes man from lower creation, and which may be designated as "reason." The belief that, with the removal of "reason," not man but only animal is left may seem obvious to the point of being banal; yet the neglect or actual discarding of this commonplace was to plunge European philosophy, by the close of the eighteenth century, into a disunity which was without parallel in its entire history, and from which it has shown no genuine sign of emergence.

I affirm [said Erasmus], that, as the instinct of the dog is to hunt, of the bird to fly, of the horse to gallop, so the natural bent of man is to philosophy and right and conduct. . . . What is the proper nature of man? Surely it is to live the life of reason, for reason is the peculiar prerogative of man.[14]

From the moral exercise of this faculty, aided by classical authority and religious purpose, insight into the universal may be attained; and the grasp of the absolute standard which that insight affords is, for the humanist, the sure and indeed the only means of estimating the simultaneously real, beautiful, and good, and of evaluating the material reflection of these universals in both human ethics and art.

To know the ideally good with genuine conviction is to insure the fulfillment of it in judgment and act. Humanism, from Plato through the Renaissance, in general subscribes to the contention that what may be called the "will" is dependent upon the "reason," and is determined by it. To know the good is to do it: not to do it arises from a misapprehension of precisely what the good is; it may arise, for example, from the belief that another course of action is preferable or at least more pleasant for oneself — a belief

[14] *De Pueris Instituendis,* in *Erasmus Concerning the Aim and Method of Education* (ed. Woodward, Cambridge, 1904), p. 190.

which implies an ignorant confusion of the good with pleasure. The prevalence and strength of this ethical principle in later medieval and Renaissance thought may be illustrated by the fact that the word "dunce" was coined in honor of the extreme followers of Duns Scotus, whose philosophy of "voluntarism" maintained that the will is not dependent at all upon the reason. In the opinion of many of the opponents of Scotus, to say that the will was independent of a rational guide was not, in the final analysis, to maintain that the will was "free": it was rather to admit as an ultimate conclusion that the will is so completely determined by the chain of fluctuating forces and circumstances in the material world that ethical judgment of motives is impossible. Indeed, the will is free only *through* its dependence on the intellect. Because the will follows the intellectual conviction of what is good — and such a conviction implies not an acquiescent half-conception but a firm and vital grasp of the good — all evaluation and all ethical action which proceeds from that evaluation are, in the traditional phrase, *sub ratione boni.*

VI

The exercise of reason, therefore, and the proper use by it of experience, of classical philosophy, and of humanistic studies in general, result in forming the temper and tone of character, the standard of judgment, purposes, and conduct, and the subsequent abidance by that standard, which together constitute the fulfillment of man's "nature." Thus Erasmus could insist that "Nature hath endued man with knowledge of liberal sciences and a fervent desire of knowledge: which thing as it doth most specially withdraw man's wit from all beastly wildness, so hath it a special grace *to get and knit together love and friendship.*" [15]

Such a fulfillment of his ideal "nature" will not suffer a man to incline towards whatever would deprive him of the companionship of the noble and the rationally good in art or conduct. He

[15] *Against War* (ed. Einstein, Boston: 1907), pp. 8–9.

carries within him his own standard not as a dogma to which to adhere in letter, but as a living intuition; indeed Plato and Aristotle would not have understood the divorce between reason and intuition which seventeenth-century mathematical rationalism was to encourage and European romanticism was generally to accept.

The man who possesses this insight, at once rational and moral, is to be considered, Aristotle had maintained, as the arbiter in all questions of aesthetic taste and of ethics. With Renaissance humanists, and especially with those neo-classic critics, such as Dennis, who are relatively close to the humanistic spirit, this contention is increasingly applied with historical pertinence as well: rational determination of the absolute and ideally good in taste and morality is to be facilitated and made more authoritative by the study of the preferences and the conduct of the best in all ages, and especially in classical antiquity.

Some indication was earlier given of the more radical ramifications in Renaissance and neo-classic criticism of the classical and humanistic principles of decorum, of proportion, and of the ethical purpose of the poet. Similarly, from the humanistic emphasis upon reason as man's distinctive faculty and as his means of contact with the universe, there arise in the Renaissance and culminate in neo-classicism an optimism, based on a confidence in the order of the universe and in man's ability to conceive and abide by that order, and also, with an accompanying trust that only "method" is needed to arrive at and reflect that order, a widespread interest in method itself. "From heavenly harmony," wrote Dryden, "this universal frame began"; and as reason underlies the law and order of nature, human reason is an extension and mirroring of that universal harmony. "Nature," said Dennis, paraphrasing D'Aubignac, is "that Rule and Order and Harmony which we find in the visible Creation," while "Reason is the very same throughout the invisible Creation. For Reason is Order and the Result of Order." [16] Not to conceive and act aright is simply a failure to perceive, by rational

[16] *Advancement and Reformation of Modern Poetry* (1701), pp. [14–15].

means, the nature of order: "nothing can be irregular either in our Conceptions or our Actions, any further than it swerves from Rule, that is, from Reason." [17] Consequently, as Pope stated,

> All Nature is but art, unknown to thee;
> All chance, direction, which thou canst not see;
> All discord, harmony not understood;
> All partial evil, universal good.

Renaissance humanism had been characterized by faith based upon reason. The eighteenth century, Mr. Whitehead has said, is "an age of reason based upon faith" — "a faith in the order of nature," of the universal frame.[18] The statement is especially an adequate definition of the movement which was known as Deism, and which was peculiarly indicative of a prevailing temper of the Enlightenment. It is true not only of such thorough-going rationalists as Samuel Clarke, John Toland, or Matthew Tindal, who strove to make their blueprints of the universe "reasonably" and even mathematically demonstrable. Its reflection is strong even in the "moral sense" deists such as Shaftesbury and his prolific following: characteristic are the very names of such Shaftesburyan poems as Henry Brooke's *Universal Beauty* (1728–1735), John Gilbert Cooper's *The Power of Harmony* (1745), James Harris's *Concord* (1751), and a bevy of other poems with such titles as *Order* or *Design and Beauty*. It is significant that the English neo-classic figures who most strenuously combat this easy optimism — Swift, Bishop Butler, and Johnson — are men who are at once distinguished by an intense religious conviction and by a genuinely classical conception of the problem of evil inherent in the empirical world.

Accompanying the optimistic generalization that the "rules" which reason discovers are "nature methodized," was an essentially unclassical interest in "method" itself. The exemplification of this interest may be generally described as twofold. It is shown

---

[17] *Grounds of Criticism in Poetry* (1704), p. 5.
[18] *Science and the Modern World* (1925), p. 83.

in a somewhat excessive and increasingly academic investigation of the rules which should comprise method, and in an attempt
to apply them, whether in aesthetics, morality, or theology, with
almost mathematical precision. A further manifestation, above all
in British empiricism, was a growing attention to the nature of the
reasoning and "methodizing" faculty itself — a tendency which,
by the middle of the eighteenth century, was to culminate in a
marked skepticism about both reason and method, and was therefore to furnish an argumentative basis for romanticism. Many of
the varying English neo-classic conceptions of what constitutes
aesthetic judgment, except where they are directly classical in
origin, may be said to have been largely determined by the paths
which the investigation of "method" pursued. In addition, an
inevitable antagonism to this excessive methodizing became increasingly marked, with a resulting emphasis upon feeling; but
this emphasis was to receive small philosophical support until its
mighty ally, British psychological empiricism, abandoned "reason"
for subjective "sentiment."

CHAPTER II.

NEO–CLASSIC DEVELOPMENTS AND REACTIONS

Classicism assumed that the ideal or universal which comprises the absolute standard of taste may be known by the direct use of man's ethical reason; it was often the contention of neo-classic rationalism that this standard was to be known and achieved by a proper use of method and of rules. The importance of aesthetic rules, as they were evolved by seventeenth-century French criticism and reiterated in English neo-classicism, does not reside simply in the assistance which they may render in the creation and understanding of art: they are themselves a part, rather, of an infallible and universal rule of order, and are thus, as Charles Gildon wrote, among "the Laws of Nature, which always acts with Uniformity, renews them incessantly, and gives them a perpetuate Existence." [1]

An academic formulation and respect for rules had already begun to flourish in Italian art and criticism of the sixteenth century. In opposition to the Reformation, an extensive catechism of faith, consisting of unalterably regulative laws and theories, had issued from the Council of Trent (1545–1563); and the almost official encouragement and sanction which this triumph of dogmatic rule gave to academic regulation in subsequent Italian art amply justifies the traditional designation of this art as "Trentine." Throughout the middle of the sixteenth century, Vasari and the Italian "Mannerists," attempting to follow Michelangelo, Raphael, and the Venetians, placed their confidence in learning and theorizing upon the technical mechanics which had been employed during the High

---

[1] *Complete Art of Poetry* (1718), I, 135.

Renaissance. The codification of rules which accompanied this belief that taste was to be formed primarily by an extensive theoretical education was further extended during the early seventeenth century by the "eclectic" or "academic" school which was ushered in by the Caracci brothers and by Guido Reni, and which came to an unexpected flowering in the painting of Poussin. Similarly, Italian critics, during the sixteenth century, attempted to construct a series of rules by studying the example of classical literature: the formulation of the "unities" and of other doctrines of decorum by Scaliger, Cintio, and Castelvetro, among others, was cited in the previous chapter; and in a similar vein was the deliberate attempt by the French poets who are known as the *Pléiade* to systematize and abide by the rules they discovered in the practice of the ancients.

The further influence of this emphasis on aesthetic rule, and of the concern for intricacy and complication of form to which it gave rise, may be illustrated by the extent to which it also joined forces and in some respects governed the character of the broad movement which is called the "baroque." An aspiration for the monumental and the dramatic, which in painting and sculpture had been strongly encouraged by the example of Michelangelo, became more marked as the seventeenth century approached; and the rapid growth of the importance of the stage itself is somewhat indicative of its literary repercussions. To the customary classical purposes of poetry, instruction and delight, Minturno had contributed "admiration"; and even Dryden was later to maintain that the poet's function is, "above all, to move admiration (which is the delight of serious plays)." The dramatic and almost flamboyant exfloreation of form which accompanied the monumentality of the baroque became increasingly determined, in at least some of its directions, by rigid canons for both the general structural outline of a production and the subordinate outlines of its parts. The centrally controlled but elaborate complication by rule which resulted from this combination may be typified at its crest by the architecture and landscaping of Versailles, by the dramas of Corneille, and later, of course, by the music of Bach and Handel.

The neo-classic merging of aesthetic rules into a part of the infallible machinery of universal order was propelled indirectly by the growth of seventeenth- and early eighteenth-century rationalistic philosophy, and also by a direct turning to philosophy by criticism in order to justify aesthetic rules upon the widest possible grounds. The extent to which philosophy itself had universalized the conception of rule may be illustrated by the hardening of the common Renaissance belief in hierarchical order into a widespread confidence, as Mr. Lovejoy has shown, in a "great chain of being," in which every variety of creature has its specific and rigidly determined "link." Similarly, from the frequent Renaissance attitude towards God as a kind of universal "architect," there issued an occasional conception, particularly common in deistic writing, of God as an architect whose plans were determined by a preëxisting series of rational regulations, the comprehension of which almost permits man to meet God on terms of mutual understanding. Thus the deist, Matthew Tindal, as Sir Leslie Stephen has said, speaks as though "he had been present when the contract, upon which was founded the Law of Nature, was drawn up and signed by the respective parties; and he can define with the utmost accuracy the reciprocal rights and duties of man and man's Creator."

Such an attitude, which helped to evoke from contemporary satires and sermons an energetic attack on intellectual pride, is an extreme manifestation of the broad rationalistic conviction that the "law of nature" is a codification of unalterable but intelligible rules which find their closest parallel in mathematics. It is characteristic that, of the three outstanding continental philosophers of the seventeenth century, Descartes and Leibniz were mathematicians, while Spinoza adopted a rigid system of geometrical axiom and proof for the demonstration of his metaphysics and ethics.

Descartes may be taken as a preëminent herald of this mathematical aspiration. Having found a method whereby geometry could be combined with algebra, and thus having revealed that in the last analysis the two were essentially one, he was tempted to assume that problems of whatever sort could all be solved by one method if they were approached mathematically. To employ this approach, as it is advanced in the famous *Discours de la Méthode* (1637), one has only to exclude all except such "clear and distinct ideas" as are self-evident: the problem then becomes merely a matter of arranging and methodizing these ideas in proper order. The imagination, because its contribution is necessarily gleaned from sense-perceptions, must be strenuously prevented from interfering: the attempt to conceive rational truths by means of it is impossible; and those, for example, "who try to imagine God or the soul are like those who would use eyes to hear sounds or smell odors." The confidence that reason has ample materials from which to work, that order is completely intelligible to man, and that method alone is necessary to discern it, may be said to have become a widespread belief by the close of the seventeenth century; and even Dennis, who emphasized the importance of evoking the passions in art, confessed that the end of logical thought "is to bring Order, and Rule, and Method to our conceptions, the want of which causes most of our Ignorance, and all our Errors."

The Cartesian assumption, of course, leaves unanswered the primary question whether all reality is capable of being proved mathematically or indeed whether it has to be proved thus. From the excluding of all ideas except those which are absolutely "clear and distinct" to the reason, and from the forbidding of any conclusion on the basis of them except that which is abstractly demonstrable in a manner analogous to mathematics, there issued stranger results than Descartes could have foreseen. It was not the historical evolution of Cartesianism but rather its primary assumptions which strongly affected neo-classic aesthetic criticism; but this evolution marks at least one distinctive trend in Enlightenment philosophy, and is also somewhat symbolic of many of the limitations and consequences of mathematical rationalism which emerged in early eighteenth-century thought generally. For from its demand for an essentially mechanical explanation, and from its condemnation as distorted and untrustworthy of whatever may be known through the medium of feeling, imagination, or even direct empirical experience, Cartesian mathematicism eventually had to discard as unknowable — and therefore, since the mathematical reason is infallible, as nonexistent — all except the mechanical itself; and at the end of this evolution, as M. Gilson has shown, emerged French materialism. Since Descartes, for example, had not succeeded very well in mathematically demonstrating beyond doubt the existence and nature of the soul or the mind, his followers, proceeding on the same basis, drew the inevitable conclusion that there was none — a conclusion which Descartes would have apprehensively disowned. In his *L'Homme Machine* (1748), a book for which Frederick the Great wrote an enthusiastic eulogy, La Mettrie extolled Descartes as "the first who perfectly demonstrated animals to be meer machines. Now, after so important a discovery, a discovery which shews so much penetration in the discoverer, . . . how can we avoid showing an indulgent and forgiving temper to all his errors." [2] In fact, he condescendingly adds, Descartes' postulation of a soul may not have been an error after all, but rather an expert and shrewd "stroke of policy, a piece of finesse, to make the Divines swallow the poison which was concealed!" As for man, said La Mettrie wistfully: "*There* is an enlightened machine!" "If a man would rather be a machine," said Dr. Johnson, "I cannot argue with him." Indeed, every man is a "watch," wrote Du Marsais in the papers he bequeathed to the D'Holbach club of *philosophes;* and the true Cartesian philosopher is not only "a human machine, like any other man," but is also "a watch that is capable of winding itself." One may note, by the way, that on the basis of these papers, the earnest Baron D'Holbach at once busied himself with an article on whether or not religion is "useful in politics"; for Du

[2] *Man a Machine* (anon. Eng. transl., 1750), p. 75.

Marsais had also proved that "Society is the only divinity in the world which the *philosophe*" — that is to say, the self-winding watch — "recognizes!" [3]

II

Although he is reported to have said that Descartes "cut the throat of poetry," Boileau's *Art Poétique* (1674) has been called, and with some justice, "the Cartesian *Discours de la Méthode* of French poetry"; and his watchword, "Aimez donc la raison," exhorted the writer or critic to consult, not a disconnected body of inherited regulations, but a framework of universalized rational law. Characteristic is the triumphant assertion of Gildon, who once considered himself a deist, that his teachers, Boileau, Dacier, Rapin, and Bossu did not, as had the Italians, simply repeat or formulate individual rules; they presented rather, "the solid Doctrine they have drawn from [the rules], and the insuperable *Reasons* on which they are founded"; and ability in aesthetic judgment, he emphasizes, is in proportion to the extent that one knows and applies this doctrine.

The famous and rather chaotic critical war between the Ancients and the Moderns reflects the more extreme aspects of this tendency: the Moderns in general felt, not that the Ancients were too bound by rules, but that they were not correct enough in their observance of them. Italian critics, during the sixteenth century, had censured Homer's failure to observe scrupulously some of their newly-enunciated laws of decorum; and Castelvetro had felt certain that Aristotle had failed to grasp the exquisite rationality of the "unity of time." D'Aubignac, somewhat later, formulated as a critical rule the growing French use of the *liaison des scènes,* at which Dryden on one occasion mildly jested, and according to which the various scenes of a drama were connected by the presence at the beginning of a scene of an actor

[3] F. Tamisier, *Du Marsais* (Marseille: 1862), and W. H. Wickwar, *Baron D'Holbach* (1935), p. 70.

who had been on the stage at the close of the preceding one. D'Aubignac, however, was willing to permit an interlinkage by having an actor appear at the opening of a scene who was either "looking for" a character present in the previous one or who had heard a noise that had been made during it. Racine may well have been justified when he complained that the audience, at the opening performance of his comedy, apprehensively wished to laugh according to the rules.

The critical controversy over the Ancients and the Moderns was given renewed impetus in the 1680's by the French critics, Perrault, and Fontenelle; and, although Boileau and Dacier, among others, had modestly sided with the ancients, Pascal's attempt to point out that there is a difference between scientific and humane pursuits, and that the scientific developments since classical antiquity did not necessarily imply progress in the arts, proved to be little more than a voice crying in a wilderness of academic legislation. We may remember that Gulliver, during his trip to Glubbdubdrib, was allowed to summon from the dead whomever he wished to see, and "proposed that Homer and Aristotle might appear at the head of all their commentators; but these were so numerous that some hundreds were forced to attend in the court and outward rooms of the palace. . . . I soon discovered that both of them were perfect strangers to the rest of the company, and had never seen or heard of them before." In England, Thomas Rymer believed that, in the rationalization of critical theory at least, the moderns were superior to the ancients; and he energetically defended such artificial decorums as that which forbade the characters in a drama killing each other unless their ranks were suitable to "the laws of the Duel" — a decorum which he listed in his table of contents as "Who and Who May Kill One Another with Decency." The faithful but not quite comprehending English henchman of the French critics, Charles Gildon, thought that they were in general more correct than Aristotle or Horace, and that they had effectively established an unshakeable standard of taste; and in his *For the Modern Poets against the Ancients* (1694), he tried to show that modern poets, too, had more "judgment" and were less likely to be "guilty of absurdities" in breaking the rules. Even John Dennis felt that the best of modern poetry was superior: his estimate, however, was not based solely on "correctness," and as his outstanding example he chose Milton rather than the occasionally cited Romulus and Remus of English "correctness," Waller and Denham, whose stylistic elegance he considered "sophisticated and debauched."

By the last quarter of the seventeenth century, indeed, the universalization of aesthetic rules in general by French criticism had extended to England, although it was far less dominant there than in the country of its origin. The critical application in England of the French rationalistic spirit, and its accompanying limitation of the province of art to the city and the court, may almost be said to begin as early as D'Avenant's preface to *Gondibert* (1650) and Hobbes's answer to that preface; and within another thirty years, several translations and imitations of Boileau had been made. The verse-essays on poetry by Roscommon and Mulgrave reiterated the standpoint of Boileau, and, as Granville said in his *Essay upon Unnatural Flights in Poetry* (1701),

> Roscommon first, then Mulgrave rose, like light,
> To clear our darkness and to guide our flight;
> With steady judgment, and in lofty sounds,
> They gave us patterns, and they set us bounds.

So firmly grounded are the rules in purely rational principles, thought Rymer, that even learning was unnecessary to the poet or the reader; "common sense alone suffices." The essence of mathematical thought is the *a priori* reasoning on self-evident principles from self-evident premises; and the rules are quite as "convincing and clear as any demonstration of Mathematics." The extremity of mechanical regulation may be exemplified by such handbooks of rules as Edward Bysshe's *Art of English*

Poetry (1702) or Gildon's *Laws of Poetry* (1721), the latter of which led a contemporary poet to boast that he did not

> vainly buy what Gildon sells,
> Poetic buckets for dry wells.

Gildon, who thought that rules were "more essential to Poetry than to any other Art or Science," was also hopeful that even more of them might be added to the poetic catechism after the model of Newton's mathematical discoveries. Some years later, a critic of even less eminence believed this hope had been fulfilled, and triumphantly proclaimed that at last "dramatic poetry stands upon the same footing with our noble system of Newtonian philosophy." [4] —

> Nature and Nature's laws lay hid in night;
> God said, "Let Newton be!" and all was light.

And as late as the middle of the century, Joseph Warton complained of "that geometrical, and systematical spirit so much in vogue, which has spread itself from the sciences even into polite literature." [5]

III

Cartesian rationalism, in its emphasis upon the mathematically demonstrative, may be said to have inculcated into extremer neo-classic criticism a rigid distinction between whatever imaginative and emotional response a human being may have, and what one should think as a strictly rational creature. Both the imagination and the passions had been subordinated by humanistic classicism to a rational insight into the decorum of the ideal; but a constant though subordinate use of them in ethical teaching and in both aesthetic creation and understanding or taste had generally been taken for granted as indispensable. Something of this assumption is

[4] William Guthrie, *Essay upon English Tragedy* (1747), p. 6.
[5] *Essay on the Writings and Genius of Pope* (1756), I, 204.

certainly present in the more outstanding neo-classic writers.
Boileau had cautioned the poet:

> In all you write, observe with care and art
> To move the passions, and incline the heart;

and both Dryden and Pope reiterated and often put into practice
this admonition. But as reason became increasingly restricted in its
connotation, and was directed less to a comprehensive ethical conception of man's nature and function than to ordered construction
on the basis of the abstractly logical and the mathematically self-
evident, the imagination and the passions could be regarded by many
writers as little more than hindrances to proper rational exercise. In
keeping with this position was a tendency, common enough in classicism but somewhat more pronounced in neo-classic rationalism,
to regard the essential creative faculty of the artist as "invention"
— a faculty which, in its "imitation" of nature, conceives the design and order of its production; and accordingly, even more
strictly than in Renaissance criticism, fancy or the imagination
was assigned rather to the adornment of this structural outline by
figurative or symbolic expression. The superlative "invention" of
Homer, said Pope, in the preface to his translation of the *Iliad*,
is best exemplified in the construction of the ordered "fable" or
outline, "which Aristotle calls the *Soul of poetry*." The fable of
the *Iliad* is

the *Anger of* Achilles, the most short and single Subject that ever was
chosen by any Poet. Yet this he has supplied with a vaster Variety of
Incidents and Events, and crowded with a greater Number of Councils,
Speeches, Battles, and Episodes of all kinds, than are to be found even
in those Poems whose Schemes are of the utmost Latitude and Irregularity.[6]

It is true that, upon at least one occasion, Dryden included "invention" under the heading of "imagination," assigning the task
of the disposition of material to "fancy":

[6] Preface to the *Iliad* (1715), in *Prose Works* (ed. Ault, 1936), p. 226.

The first happiness of the poet's imagination is properly invention . . .: the second is fancy, or the variation, deriving, or moulding of that thought, as the judgment represents it as proper to the subject; the third is elocution. . . .[7]

And Pope later associated Homer's "invention" with "imaginative force":

It is to the Strength of this amazing Invention we are to attribute that unequall'd Fire and Rapture, which is so forcible in *Homer*, that no Man of a true Poetical Spirit is Master of himself while he reads him. . . . The Reader is hurry'd out of himself by the Force of the Poet's Imagination.[8]

But by many critics "invention" seems to have been regarded largely as a rational procedure: whatever contribution the imagination had to make was to be confined to ornamenting in exact accordance with the decorum of the general design and of its component parts — a decorum which is ascertained and exhibited in art by rational grasp and the proper employment of rule; and, because they comprise the codification of the truths of nature and the means of knowing them, "a strict attendance to the *Rules of Nature and Reason*," said Gildon, "can never embarrass or clogg an Author's Fancy, but rather enlarge and extend it." The exclusive employment of the imagination itself in the "invention" of the fable will only lead to an improbable and indeed false representation of the rational chain of circumstance and meaning which lies behind and indeed constitutes "nature." Despite the popularity of Spenser in early eighteenth-century England, neo-classic critics continually cited the poetic romances of the Middle Ages and of the Renaissance as characteristic of the inventive use in structural form of "fancy" rather than "reason." The writers of such romances, said one critic,

were seized with an irregular Poetick phrenzy, and having Decency and Probability in Contempt, fill'd the World with endless Absurdities. . . .

[7] *Essays* (ed. cit.), I, 15.
[8] *Prose Works*, p. 224.

While this sort of Writing was in fashion, the Imaginations of the modern Poets . . . imbib'd a strong tincture of the Romantick Contagion, which corrupted their Taste, and occasion'd their neglect of Probability.[9]

Similarly, though the figurative adornment of art may evoke emotional reaction, the essential form, which is rationally portrayed in art, must also be rationally known; and that response to "invention" and the comprehension of its significance which comprise aesthetic taste are less the function of feeling than of "judgment" — a faculty or exercise of mind which, in most English criticism since the middle of the seventeenth century, had been diametrically opposed to "enthusiasm" and "fancy." For "that which we call Taste in Writing," said Dennis, "is nothing but a fine Discernment of Truth."

But even in the use of language and ornament, imaginative fervor, except by a few writers, was hardly regarded as a desirable end in this age when

> . . . Phoebus touch'd the Poet's trembling Ear
> With one supreme Commandment, *Be thou Clear.*

The great reformation of English prose during the latter half of the seventeenth century — an alteration which has not been over-estimated in either its extent or rapidity — was accompanied by a continual critical encouragement which was also to leave some effect on poetic theory and practice. One of the first measures taken in the founding of the Royal Society during the English Civil War by a group of men who wished to "breathe a free air . . . without being engaged in the passions and madness of that dismal Age" was the decision to make their language denotative rather than connotative: to divest it, as Thomas Sprat stated in his famous *History of the Royal Society* (1667), of "those spacious *Tropes* and *Figures* of imaginative writing which result in

[9] Sir Richard Blackmore, "Essay on Epick Poetry," *Essays upon Various Subjects* (1716–17), I, 31–32.

only mists and uncertainties." "Nature" is to be regarded as only the rationally self-evident; and in order to "separate the knowledge of *Nature* from the Colours of Rhetorick, the devices of Fancy," it was necessary to be "arm'd against all the enchantments of *Enthusiasm*." The members of the Society

have therefore been most rigorous in putting in execution the only Remedy that can be found for this extravagance: and that has been, a constant Resolution, to reject all the amplifications, digressions, and swellings of style: to return back to the primitive purity, and shortness, when men deliver'd so many *things*, almost in an equal number of *words*. They have exacted from all their members, a close, naked, natural way of speaking; positive expressions; clearness; a native easiness: bringing all things as near the Mathematical plainness, as they can.[10]

A somewhat similar aim is stressed in the various contemporary discussions of sermon-writing, such as those of John Eachard and Joseph Glanvil. "A man," said Dryden, "is to be cheated into Passion, but to be reason'd into Truth." Characteristic of the same standpoint is Swift's "Letter to a Young Clergyman," in which emotional eloquence is condemned as evoking only the most temporary and unstable response:

I do not see how this talent of moving the passions can be of any great use toward directing Christian men in the conduct of their lives. . . . I am confident the strongest eloquence of that kind will leave few impressions upon any of our spirits deep enough to last till the next morning, or rather to the next meal.[11]

This stylistic conviction, especially as it concerned religious writing, both helped to augment and in turn received an ethical encouragement and qualification from the late seventeenth-century reverberations of the trend of Renaissance moral thought which is loosely designated as "neo-stoicism." Such Renaissance moral writing as had been composed in the stoical vein had tradi-

---

[10] Pp. 53, 62, 113.
[11] *Prose Works* (ed. Temple Scott, 1897–1908), III, 205.

tionally tended to regard emotion of whatever sort as liable to deflect man from the path to virtue and contentment. The works attacking "enthusiasm" by such writers as Meric Casaubon and Henry More forecast the direction that neo-stoicism was to take as the eighteenth century approached. Francis Bragge, for example, who was canon of Lincoln, wrote for his flock a characteristic *Practical Treatise of the Regulation of the Passions* (1708), in which he attempted to devise methods for governing almost any variety of feeling. For not only zeal or enthusiasm but even the charitable and benevolent passions, which the Shaftesburyans were soon to extol, became viewed as sand in the machinery of man's moral character: the goal of neo-stoicism was unimpassioned thought, and moderation and prudence in action. As among Swift's Houyhnhnms, its "grand maxim is, to cultivate reason, and to be wholly governed by it."

The general moralistic and scientific antagonism towards stylistic fervor and enthusiasm had, of course, its accompanying parallel — a parallel which may be overstressed — in a fashionable though not completely dominant critical attitude towards the language of poetry. For even in its legitimate function of adding ornament to the more primary and rationally conceived outline of a composition, the imagination should be restrained from any exuberance which may, by a breach of rule or by an independent accentuation of a part, distract attention from the whole. Restraint in the use of metaphor and simile is often urged; the very title, for example, of Granville's *Essay upon Unnatural Flights in Poetry* (1701) is indicative. The rules of Horace, said Waller,

> will our superfluous branches prune,
> Give us new rules and keep our harp in tune;
> Direct us how to back the wingèd horse,
> Favor his flight and moderate his force.

The repose and serenity which generally characterize classical art and literature were less a conscious stylistic intention than they were a result, an external manifestation, of the larger attempt to present all of the potentialities of the ideal or the universal in a harmonious grace and to subdue them to a general consonance. Many neo-classic writers and painters occasionally lack a certain genuineness from having directed their gaze to the external accompaniments rather than the internal intention of classical art, and from having regarded stylistic restraint as a deliberate and paramount aim; and one is sometimes tempted to say, with Roy Campbell, "They use the snaffle and the curb, all right, But where's the bloody horse?"

The conscious attempt to achieve a confinement and regulation of style as an end in itself was supported not only by a restriction in the connotation of "reason," but also by an accompanying restriction of what constitutes decorum. Neo-classicism retained the traditional classical conviction that the language of literature was less the limited vocabulary of the uneducated than the somewhat more articulate language of the educated. But it did not too often distinguish between the decorum of the ideal, as held in successive generations, and the artificial decorums of behavior and speech in the polite society of its own day. The critical defense of the famous "poetic diction" of much neo-classic English poetry occasionally reveals this confusion of ideal and contemporary social decorum; and even in the latter half of the eighteenth century critics often continued to admit that

Many words there are in every tongue, which are not used, except by illiterate persons, or on very familiar occasions, or in order to express what the decorum of polite society requires that we conceal: and these may be called *mean words*, and are never to be introduced in sublime description, in elegant writing, or on any solemn or serious topick.[12]

The results, of course, were often disastrous. "She perceiveth," states the last chapter of Proverbs, "that her merchandise is good: her candle goeth not out by night. She layeth her hands to the

---

[12] James Beattie, *Dissertations Moral and Critical* (1783), p. 649.

spindle, and her hands hold the distaff." In the Biblical "translations" of Francis Fawkes, the passage reads:

> With joy her goodly merchandise she views,
> And oft till morn her pleasing work pursues,
> The spindle twirls obedient to her tread,
> Round rolls the wheel, and spins the ductile thread.

Or again, in the Song of Deborah appear the simple words: "He
asked for water, and she gave him milk. . . . At her feet he
bowed, he fell, he lay down; at her feet he bowed, he fell. . . ."
The decorous touch of Fawkes produced the rendition:

> She ask'd refreshment from the limpid wave,
> The milky beverage to the chief she gave:
> He drank, he slept extended on the floor,
> She smote the warrior, and he wak'd no more.

Not a few neo-classic critics were aware, like Sir Richard Blackmore, that "too scrupulous an exactness" in the propriety of diction and metaphor "enervates the expression"; but Blackmore's
own Pegasus, like that of many another, had clipped wings, and
adequately deserved Pope's parody:

> Lest stiff, and stately, void of fire or force,
> You limp, like Blackmore, on a Lord Mayor's horse.

Yet the vitiating effect of neo-classic poetic diction at its worst
has been more often emphasized than the advantages that often
accrued from such a genuinely skillful use of it as is found in Dryden or in Pope. The primary stylistic aims, said John Hughes in
an essay *Of Style* (1698), should be propriety in the choice of
words — a propriety to be determined by the language of people
who "speak well and without affectation"; elegance, or the use
of only such figures of speech as are rationally suitable to the subject they illustrate; a smoothness and decorum in the very sound
of the words, sentences, and meter; and, above all, perspecuity,

since an initial purpose of all writing is facility of communication. If the first two received occasional abuse, the latter two attained a fruition in neo-classic writing which is not easy to parallel in English. Indeed, all the aims which Hughes instances, and which are relatively characteristic of those urged in most neo-classic stylistic theory, are fundamentally classical. They ceased to be classical in either criticism or practice only when the primary law of humanistic decorum, the portrayal of the universal, was breached: when, that is to say, these stylistic intentions were regarded as almost sufficient ends in themselves, or when they were subjected to the authority of a prematurely generalized rationalistic code or to the satisfaction of social demands and fashions which were wholly transitory in character.

IV

The general mathematicism of the late seventeenth century, states Mr. Whitehead, was concerned with abstractions, and with "eliciting from them clear-cut demonstrative trains of reasoning, entirely satisfactory so long as it is those abstractions which you want to think about"; and its fallacy lay in "the taking as real of something, whether a physical thing or a scientific conception, that has been abstracted from reality for special purposes of thought." [13] Any essential element disregarded or excluded by a premature generalization has inevitably rankled and demanded recognition; and the restriction of "reason" to logical abstraction, accompanied by the exclusion of other aspects of mind which had found a place in the broad classical conception of ethical insight, was counterbalanced by an increasing emphasis upon feeling, sentiment, or instinct as the basis of taste. The dichotomy which the neo-classic rationalist had tended to make between "reason" and any aspect whatsoever of imagination and feeling had become sufficiently prevalent so that those who urged another basis for taste were often equally extreme in maintaining emotion as its

[13] *Science and the Modern World* (1925), p. 79.

primary foundation, and in viewing "reason" and the employment of the rules as almost its opposite.

Throughout the seventeenth century generally, and particularly as the rules became increasingly demanding and academic in application, the conception of taste as non-rational frequently found its keynote in the phrase, *je ne sais quoi*, a phrase which was given particular currency by the *Précieuses*, and which became a modish expression in both France and England by the close of the century. The critics who inclined towards the rather vague outlook which was represented by this phrase, and who had little general connection with each other except an antipathy to rules, have occasionally been called the "School of Taste." The designation is justified to the extent that the critical word, "taste," which had been popularized in Spain, was in general used as synonymous with a subjective *je ne sais quoi* sentiment until almost the middle of the eighteenth century. No one denied the existence of such a sentiment. Dryden, for example, spoke of his preference for Juvenal rather than Horace as a result of his "own taste"; or Pope stated that the occasional breaking of a rule may achieve "a grace beyond the reach of art,"

> Which, without passing through the judgment, gains
> The heart, and all its end at once attains.

The question, then, was not whether such an emotional capacity existed but whether it was the final judge of aesthetic value. With the admission, however, that, as Montesquieu later said, "art gives the rules, and taste the exceptions," there arose the further problem of what faculty or means was to determine when the rules were to be broken and when not; and since rational rules were not applicable to this further quality, only "taste" could determine the proper occasion of its own use, and thus serve as the ultimate judge. The *je ne sais quoi* attitude towards taste, encouraged in various ways by such critics as Meré, Bouhours, Saint-Évremond, and La Bruyére, became sufficiently widespread to provoke in reply a renewed and more energetic defense of the rules, such as that which Dacier prefixed to his translation of Aristotle's *Poetics* (1692). Indeed, much of the more extreme insistence upon rules at the turn of the century may be attributed to its having been partially voiced in a spirit of defense rather than of complete confidence. Gildon, who prided himself on his severity as a taskmaster, often bewailed the contemporary lack of respect for rules, especially among his countrymen. One may suspect that his own admiration for the rules was hardly as ingrained as he would have liked, and that he protested too much even for himself; for though in calmer moods he sternly censured the "irregularity" of Shakespeare's plays, he always found to his dismay that, in reading Shakespeare, the "witchery in him" caused all remembrance of rules to "vanish away . . . as if I had never known anything of the matter."

The antipathy to rules which was expressed by the "School of Taste" was more widespread in England than on the continent; and practicing poets or dramatists, such as George Farquhar, occasionally attacked the rules as the pronouncement, not of the artist, but of commentators who were unendowed with any aesthetic capacity and who were consequently oblivious to the nature and working of the artist. Sir William Temple, who is peculiarly characteristic of the English virtuoso spirit, considered that rules could do no more than "hinder some men from being very ill Poets, but not . . . make any man a very good one." The codification of rules is symptomatic of literary "decay":

> It would be too much Mortification to these great Arbitrary Rulers among the *French* Writers or our own to observe the worthy Productions that have been formed by their Rules. . . . But to comfort them, I do not know there was any great Poet in *Greece* after the Rules of that Art layd down by *Aristotle*, nor in *Rome* after those by *Horace*, which yet none of our Moderns pretend to have out-done.

Similarly, Temple viewed askance the contemporary application to

Smoothness of Language or Style, which has at best but the Beauty of Colouring in a Picture, & can never make a good one without Spirit and Strength. The Academy set up by Cardinal *Richlieu* to amuse the Wits of that Age and Country, and divert them from raking into his politicks and Ministry, brought this in Vogue. . . .[14]

In modern poetry, Temple found little to praise except English drama, particularly Shakespeare. Indeed, one of the contributing or at least encouraging elements to the more pronounced English antipathy to rules was that England possessed a large body of creative literature which had been written long before the infiltration of French rationalistic criticism. The consciousness of this possession enabled many English writers to vent their nationalistic feelings. "These *Corneillean* Rules," said one, "are as Dissonant to the *English* Constitution of the Stage, as the *French* Slavery to our *English* liberty";[15] and similar assertions are not uncommon throughout the eighteenth century. In stressing the emotional basis of taste, the proponents of the *je ne sais quoi* attitude frequently sought to account for national variation of taste by referring it to the influence of "climate," an influence which had occasionally been cited both in classical antiquity and in the Renaissance. At least some effect of climate on aesthetic temper was taken for granted, not only by writers like Bouhours and Temple, but Dryden, Dennis, and the Abbé du Bos, who can hardly be precisely bracketed with the "School of Taste," show an awareness of it. The climatological theory became relatively common throughout the eighteenth century, and, as the works of Taine especially illustrate, was by no means abandoned in the following century.

The neo-classic "School of Taste" in England both facilitated and in turn drew encouragement from the rising popularity of the famous Greek treatise, attributed to Longinus, *On the Sublime*. The urging by Longinus of the psychological and emotional

---

[14] "Of Poetry," in *Works* (1770), III, 405, 423.
[15] Edward Filmer, *Defense of Dramatic Poetry* (1698), II, 28.

elements in the creation and understanding of art, his assumption
that art should transport as well as persuade, and his emphasis
upon boldness and grandeur of conception and upon a capacity
for the pathetic — that is to say, for the raising of the passions —
as all-important and inherent aesthetic gifts, served as something
of an authoritative rallying center for the defense of a subjective
and emotional taste. The growing vogue of Longinus in the
early eighteenth century may be illustrated by Swift's caution, in
his verses called *On Poetry: A Rhapsody*, that "a forward Crit-
ick,"

> . . . if we have not read *Longinus*,
> Will magisterially out-shine us.
> Then lest with *Greek* he over-run ye,
> Procure the Book for Love or Money.

In keeping with the prevalent neo-classic interest in forming a
just style, Longinus was at first regarded chiefly as the writer of
a stylistic essay of interest. Characteristic are the titles of the first
English translation, *Of the Height of Eloquence* (1652), and of
the second, *A Treatise of the Loftiness or Elegancy of Speech*
(1680); and it was not until 1698 that an English translator,
following Boileau, employed the word "sublime" in his title.
John Dennis, who was derisively dubbed "Sir Longinus" by some
of his contemporaries, continually dwelt on the importance of the
sublime, instancing Milton as a preëminent example of it; and,
more successfully than Boileau, Dennis occasionally made efforts
to combine the emotional basis which Longinus partially justified
with the broad exercise of reason and a discriminating employment of the rules.

But Dennis was rather an exception; and writers who exhorted
the authority of Longinus more frequently did so with the purpose of disparaging the rules. Thus, Leonard Welsted, who
translated Longinus (1712), considered that the rules are completely superfluous, and that taste is inborn and "cannot be re-

duced to a Science or taught by any set precepts"; for "poetical Reason is not the same as mathematical Reason." The object of taste is aesthetic "truth," a truth which is qualitatively rather than quantitatively measurable, and which is no less valid than that of mathematics; "but that Truth is not to be prov'd by the same Process or way of Working." Experience and knowledge are necessary for taste; and either the writer or critic must augment and direct this instinctive capacity by carrying "his Enquiries closely and carefully into Men, Manners, human nature; by frequently viewing Things, as they are in themselves . . . by being conversant with the Writings of great Poets . . . ; by studying severely the language he writes in. . . ." Yet whatever is acquired is of pertinence and use only if the capacity is there to mold it and render it instinctive. Indeed, taste in the arts rests primarily upon imaginative reaction; and "Imagination is as much a Part of Reason as is Memory or Judgment." [16] Similarly, in opposition to the occasional rationalistic censuring of the faults or divergences from the rules in a work of art, the *je ne sais quoi* critics attempted, in the spirit of Longinus, to concentrate on the "beauties" of whatever they considered: to "survey," as Pope said,

> . . . the WHOLE, nor seek slight faults to find
> Where Nature moves, and rapture warms the mind.

This attitude, indeed, was hardly confined to the "School of Taste": the insistence that the critic is concerned with "beauties" rather than "faults" was relatively common among all critics from Dryden to Johnson.

v

The history of the conception of aesthetic judgment is very closely interrelated with that of ethical theory; and, as the eighteenth century began, the relativism and emotionalism towards

[16] *Dissertation Concerning the Perfection of the English Language, the State of Poetry, &c.* (1724), in *Works* (1787), pp. 131, 137, and *passim.*

which the "School of Taste" inclined found justification in a
growing tendency of moral thought which originally issued from
the doctrine which is usually called "voluntarism," a doctrine
which maintains the will as independent of reason and knowledge. It was emphasized in the previous chapter that, in the view
of classical humanism, to know the good with sufficient conviction was to abide by it; that not to follow the good arose from
a confusion of it with some other course of action which, from lack
of a firmly held understanding, seemed more pleasantly desirable
or more convenient to the individual. The philosophy of voluntarism, which had been urged since the days of the Greek Sophists,
reappeared most prominently in some of the extreme followers of
the thirteenth-century British philosopher, Duns Scotus, who
sought to demonstrate that the will is not dependent on knowledge
but, on the contrary, is completely free and directed of itself to
the good. But with the will thus deprived of a rational guide, the
followers of Scotus were not exactly sure how the will was to
know the good; and from this uncertainty ultimately stemmed
both the social and empirical determinism and the emotional individualism, unified in origin but diverse in direction, which
largely tended to replace rationalism in European moral and aesthetic thought. At a loss to explain how the good is to be known
by the will, a few of the more extreme voluntarists who followed
Scotus, notably the French philosopher Pierre D'Ailly, concluded that the good cannot be known and evaluated at all —
that "nothing of itself is a sin" — except by the specific edict of
the church. Needless to say, if clerical edicts were not taken very
seriously, the manner in which ethical estimation was to proceed
would be placed in something of a dilemma; and this is precisely
what happened. The will, left rudderless in the empirical world,
was increasingly discovered to be determined by material circumstances.

This tendency to determinism of the will, at first found in only
a handful of writers, was greatly augmented by the revival of

Epicurean natural law in the sixteenth century, and in the succeeding century it flowered full-blown in the writings of Thomas Hobbes. The determinism of the will was of course only a step to a further conclusion; for, if the will is governed by the chain of events and forces of the empirical world, intrinsic motive or intention can hardly be blamed or praised. Any purely relative estimation of what is "good" must rest, rather, upon what is "convenient" to society; and from this conception, already so strong in Hobbes, arose both benevolent utilitarianism, with its concern for "the greatest happiness of the greatest number," and the half-mystical "Statolatry" familiar in much nineteenth-century German philosophy. Classical humanism had customarily maintained that the will is free only through its dependence on reason; with Cicero, it had regarded all that is not rational in man as ultimately only appetite; and the ironically deterministic result of the Scotist attempt to "free" the will from reason may remind us of the statement of Shakespeare's Ulysses that, with the removal of "the specialty of rule," power turns "into will, will into appetite; And appetite, a universal wolf," must "last eat up himself."

Similarly, others who followed in the voluntarist train and who were faced with the problem of how the will of itself was to know the good, independent of reason, rejected determinism and attempted to prove the existence of an innate "feeling" or "sense" which was automatically directed to the good. The keynote to this assumption, in English ethical theory, was sounded by Richard Cumberland, who, in his attempt to refute Hobbes, asserted the presence in man of an instinctive feeling to promote the common good; but the major impetus to the development of this belief was given at the beginning of the eighteenth century by the Earl of Shaftesbury, who sought to establish a cultivated "taste" as the fundamental basis of both art and morality. With an eclectic use of a few of the tenets of neo-Platonism, neo-Stoicism, and contemporary deistic theories of the universe,

Shaftesbury combined the virtuoso conception of taste and the benevolent utilitarianism of Cumberland. The order of the universe proclaims its fundamental characteristic as harmony; harmony being at once the reality and beauty of the universe, it follows that the true, the good, and the beautiful are the same, and that the perception of one is the perception of all three. Harmony reveals benevolence in the ruling Mind; and since benevolence dominates the universe, the proper and "natural" quality of man, as a part of the universe, is necessarily benevolence, which is a key both to his adaptation or happiness in the world and to his perception of what is beautiful and true — that is to say, of what is congruous or fitting in any aspect of the universe. The employment of this feeling in the aesthetic realm is "taste," and in the ethical realm a "moral sense"; but indeed the two are fundamentally the same. "In the very nature of things there must be the foundation of a wrong and a right taste, relish, or choice." The properties of this "taste" are "a noble enthusiasm," a benevolent social consciousness, and an urbane, optimistic, and harmonious "good-humour": indeed, Shaftesbury even questions "whether anything besides ill-humour can be the cause of atheism."

Systematized by Francis Hutcheson, who made its foundation even more aesthetic, the "moral sense" preached by Shaftesbury was later taken over, in an extremely modified form, by the Scottish "Common-Sense" School of the latter half of the eighteenth century. Its more immediate result, however, was a heartening impetus to the cult of "sensibility"; and one is tempted to note an almost inevitable progression from Shaftesbury through such works as de Pouilly's *Theory of Agreeable Sensations* (1748) to Sterne's famous apostrophe "Dear Sensibility! . . . Eternal fountain of our feelings! . . . — all comes from thee!" The Shaftesburyan emphasis on sentiment was soon reiterated in English belles-lettres. Its influence on English criticism, however, was hardly pronounced before the middle of the century except among critics of small caliber. It is apparent, for example, in the dialogues on aesthetic matters by George Stubbes, which were subtitled "Written in the Manner of Plato" but which had little in common with Plato except that they were written in dialogue. Or again, Tamworth Reresby, a retired soldier who sought to recoup his financial losses by a *Miscellany of Ingenious Thoughts and Reflections* (1721), maintained, as one of his "ingenious thoughts," that "fine taste" was "a natural sentiment," an instantaneously working "instinct."

A moderate but more detailed employment of Shaftesbury's conception of moral and aesthetic "taste" was furnished in the 1740's by William Melmoth, who shared a growing interest of his day in "original genius," and who thought that original "invention is depressed and genius enslaved" by imitation of the ancients. The general principles of taste reflect the harmony of the universal frame, and are divinely implanted in man; "they are common to our whole Species, and arise from that internal sense of beauty which every man, in some degree at least, evidently possesses." The attraction of the "internal sense" by beauty is or should be infallible:

There are certain forms which must necessarily fill the soul with agreeable ideas; and she is instantly determined in her approbation of them, previous to all reasoning concerning their use and convenience. It is upon these general principles, that what is called fine taste in the arts is founded; and consequently is by no means so precarious and unsettled an idea as you choose to describe it.

For all his protesting, however, Melmoth was actually less convinced than Shaftesbury of the infallibility of the "internal sense," and was aware that, once an emotional basis for taste was assumed, it was difficult to establish a standard for it; and he therefore, in keeping with traditional humanistic and neo-classic policy, added the caution that the verdicts of one's "internal sense" should be checked or assisted by "the works of those great masters, whose performances have been long and generally admired, [and who] supply a further criterion of fine taste, equally fixed and certain as that which is immediately derived from nature herself." This led Melmoth back to a consideration of the classics, with an implication that perhaps one should not be too "original" after all; for the critical rules of Aristotle and Horace were drawn from works

which have been distinguished by the uninterrupted admiration of all the more improved parts of mankind from their earliest appearance down to this present hour. For whatever, thro' a long series of ages, has been universally esteemed as best, cannot but be conformable to our just and natural ideals of beauty.[17]

A far more extreme disciple, however, was John Gilbert Cooper, whom Edmund Malone described as one of "the benevolists or sentimentalists, who were much in vogue between 1750 and 1760, and dealt in general admiration of virtue." Cooper considered that the "internal sense" which comprises taste transcends not only reason but also the imagination, and boasted that he could "make true Conjectures concerning a Man's Taste in Morals from the choice of his Pictures or the Disposition of his Gardens." The inevitable result of the exercise of taste is an "instantaneous Glow of Pleasure which thrills thro' our whole Frame." The belief that the proper effect of good taste is a "thrill" appears somewhat surprising in the light of his statement that the sedate Addison, though he betrayed "a poverty of Imagination," was "blessed with a Taste truly delicate and refined." Such a standpoint sanctioned a tendency among the benevolists to concentrate on a luxury of feeling for its own sake, a tendency which accompanied the growth of romanticism generally. Indeed, Boswell records that Cooper one day received news of his son's illness, and immediately fell into "such violent agitation . . . as to seem beyond the power of comfort. At length, however, he exclaimed, 'I'll write an Elegy.' Mr. Fitzherbert being satisfied by this, of the sincerity of his emotions, slyly said, 'Had you not

[17] *Letters of Sir Thomas Fitzosborne* (6th ed., 1763), pp. 182–183, 185–186, and *passim*.

better take a post-chaise and go and see him?'" "This, to be sure," said Dr. Johnson when he heard of it, "*finished* the affected man." Cooper would perhaps have agreed with Sophia Western, who, when her aunt asked her whether she did not enjoy weeping, answered, "I love a tender sensation, and would pay the price of a tear for it at any time." He also thought that "Women are the Fountains from whence flow the blended streams of Taste and Pleasure"; and we may remember Irving Babbitt's tart but perhaps justifiable assertion that "The ancient sophist at least made man the measure of all things. By subjecting judgment to sensibility, Rousseau may be said to have made woman the measure of all things." So harmonious is the interplay of the "internal sense" with world-order that "taste" and the external universe are almost two strings to "one Lute," the vibrations of each working in exquisite unison with those of the other. Since "Truth, Beauty and Utility are inseparable," the "internal sense" receives a "thrill" not only from the true and the beautiful but also from the useful, and is therefore humanitarian in its ultimate direction; indeed, the "most exquisite of all Sensations" is that "which the glowing Heart receives in relieving our Fellow-Creatures." [18]

Cooper, whom Johnson dubbed "the Punchinello of literature," may be cited as characteristic of the ironically vicious circle which Shaftesbury had resurrected in his attempt to combat Hobbes's doctrine that self-interest is the mainspring of human action. By postulating an innate "moral sense" which takes an acute pleasure in the beauty of the good, it could be retorted, and frequently was, that man's ethical action was therefore determined by a selfish desire for the pleasure he received in conforming to the good. By their occasional admission, moreover, of the useful as equivalent with the true and the good, the followers of Shaftesbury moved even closer into the arms of their former opponents; for, as Sir Leslie Stephen said about the "benevolists," "When

[18] *Letters Concerning Taste* (3rd ed., 1757), pp. 2, 5, 13, 26, 111, and *passim*.

utility was thus recognized as the criterion of virtue, it required but one step to admit that it was also the cause of moral approbation." It will be remembered that, to the true *philosophe*, to the "self-winding watch," that is, of Du Marsais, "Society is the only Divinity." With the disintegration of the classical and humanistic insistence on a broad rational insight into man's ethical ideal, the evolution of voluntarism, whether its doctrine was openly self-interest or whether it postulated a pleasurable "sense" as the guide, was capable of moving in almost the same direction as that of mathematical mechanism.

VI

The English neo-classic conceptions of taste, however, rested upon more than the codification of rules which seventeenth-century rationalism had formulated, or the premise of innate "sentiment" which was postulated in reaction to the increasing severity and exclusion of this rationalism. In addition to these tendencies of thought was the influence of British psychological empiricism, which, growing alongside the rationalistic interest in "method," turned upon the methodizing faculty itself. But British empiricism has traditionally been anti-rationalistic: it may be noted as early as the nominalism of William of Occam; Bacon's insistence on experience and his distrust of the abstractions and over-hasty generalizations of what Wordsworth called the "meddling intellect" are characteristic; and when Hobbes had said that "no discourse whatsoever can end in absolute knowledge of fact," he implied that direct sensory experience could bring such absolute knowledge. In keeping with this spirit, John Locke, in his famous *Essay Concerning Human Understanding* (1690), reiterated the traditional British distrust of logical syllogism and generalization, maintained that "we reason about particulars," and turned to the analysis of that which, by direct experience, could be most surely and immediately known — the reasoning process. Of all the philosophers of his day, wrote Condillac, "Locke is the only one who was not a geometer, and how far superior to others he was!" At least, not being a geometer, Locke felt no compulsion to deduce reality from a mathematical principle; indeed, he maintained that there is no experential proof of innate ideas and principles at all — if there were an innate idea of God, for example, as the Cartesians assumed, there would be no atheists. He resurrected the old comparison of the mind to a *tabula rasa*, an unwritten sheet: knowledge comes wholly from sensation or from reflection upon that sensation; ideas received from the former are "simple," and those deduced from the latter are either "complex," in which simple ideas have become unified, or else "abstract," in which elements have been removed for a special purpose of thought or generalization. As for matter, its qualities are two-fold: they are "primary," and are inseparably connected with the object — density, extension, figure, and motion; or they are "secondary," like colors, sounds, or odors, and exist solely as reactions elicited in the mind by the object.

After Locke, it was only a further step for Berkeley to consider all qualities of matter as simply ideas in the mind; and, as M. Gilson has said, "While the body was losing its Mind in France, the Mind was losing its body in Great Britain." One is reminded of the wit's remark: "No matter, never mind." Similarly, by its ultimate conclusion in Hume that the mind can know only its own isolated ideas, with no absolute confidence in the existence and nature either of the external world or of the rational validity of the mind's working, empiricism was to become a primary support to romantic criticism — as well as the basis for nineteenth- and twentieth-century relativistic criticism in general — and was to assist it in the establishment of a more subjective and emotional conception of taste. But, in its moderate form, the effect of empiricism was at first to aid some aspects of the main neo-classic critical tendency. For British empiricism, in its incipient stages, was no less opposed than rationalism to at least the "vagaries of the imagination." Characteristic are the stylistic resolutions of the Royal Society, and the belief of Hobbes that imagination is "decaying sense" — and consequently less trustworthy than non-decaying or active sensation. Similarly, the sensible Locke inveighed against "enthusiasm," opposing it to sane perception and practical induction; and his restriction of the imagination simply to the retention of ideas of sight — a restriction which Addison and others reiterated soon after — was somewhat in the vein of Hobbes. To Locke, moreover, as to Addison, ideas derived from simple sensation are valid and reliable; and knowledge can be attained, therefore, by the study of "the agreement or disagreement of our ideas." Knowledge is thus the province of "judgment"; and Locke's distinction between "wit" and "judgment" became a commonplace in English criticism for well over half a century: in the ability to

distinguish one thing from another, where there is but the least difference, consists, in a great measure, the exactness of judgment, and clearness of reason, which is to be observed in one man above another. And hence perhaps may be given some reason of that common observation, — that men who have a great deal of wit, and prompt memories, have not always the clearest judgment or deepest reason. For *wit* lying most in the assemblage of ideas, and putting those together with quickness and variety, wherein can be found any resemblance or congruity, thereby to make up pleasant pictures and agreeable visions in the fancy; *judgment*, on the contrary, lies quite on the other side, in separating carefully, one thing from another, ideas wherein can be found the least difference, thereby to avoid being misled by similitude, and by affinity to take one thing for another.[19]

Indeed, the common belief, as it continued in eighteenth-century English neo-classicism, that erroneous assertion or misleading reaction is the result of unschooled "wit" or "fancy," and that propriety of expression and valid estimation of anything accrue from the sane and careful use of "judgment," was not only substantiated by the moderate empiricism of Locke, but, with

[19] *Essay Concerning Human Understanding* (1690), Bk. II, chap. ix, ¶ 2.

this less rigorously and less mathematically absolute conception of
"judgment," it also assumed a direction which was more moderate, more psychologically loose and compromising, and more
genuinely English in character than was the attenuated rationalism which the followers of D'Aubignac, Rapin, Boileau, and
Dacier had sought to introduce and superimpose.

Except in those critics of the latter half of the eighteenth century who turned increasingly to the interrelation of subjective
feeling and the creative imagination as the basis of taste — and
somewhat even in them — this moderately empirical conception
of "judgment," with varying nuances which its very indefinite-
ness admitted, came to constitute for most English neo-classicism
the faculty of taste; and it took on as well a capacity for instinctive and immediate application which continental neo-classic rationalism had tended to divorce from abstract reason. The word
"taste" itself became broadened to include, not an unschooled
and innately trustworthy feeling, but a far wider capacity of
judgment, which is augmented and directed by experience and
by learning, and which in time may acquire an almost intuitional
sagacity in its objective insight.

Among the various neo-classic ramifications of this loose but
essentially English conception was one which was in many ways
close to the general classical attitude towards ethical and aesthetic
judgment, and which was certainly combined with an energetic
reassertion of basically classical and humanistic ideals. The consolidation of this tendency is best and most comprehensively exemplified in the writings of Sir Joshua Reynolds and, especially,
of Samuel Johnson.

CHAPTER III.

JOHNSON AND REYNOLDS
THE PREMISE OF GENERAL NATURE

It was his labour [said Johnson of Socrates] to turn philosophy from the study of [external] nature to speculations upon life; but the innovators whom I oppose are turning off attention from life to nature. They seem to think, that we are placed here to watch the growth of plants, or the motion of the stars. Socrates was rather of opinion, that what we had to learn was, how to do good, and avoid evil.[1]

If Socrates be considered the greatest and most exemplary of humanists, Johnson himself must be placed high in that company; and it would hardly be temerity to state that, in some respects, Johnson is both a Christian and a very English Socrates. At least the humanistic credo, combined as it often was in the Renaissance with a fervent assertion of Christian principles, found one of its last and one of its most vigorous exponents in Johnson; and, if we except occasional statements made in general conversation or elicited under the pressure of oral argument, almost all that he combated may, in some degree, be viewed as aberrations from the humanistic tradition. Like Swift, he opposed an easy optimism, and, in direct contrast with the disciples of Shaftesbury, showed a genuinely classical recognition of the very real problem of evil inherent in the material world. He considered that what is best and most representative in man is not his own "original" feelings as an individual and least of all the inclinations which the fashions of his own locality and time prompt or sanction, but rather his capacity to attain a rational grasp of the ideal and unchanging

[1] Johnson, Life of Milton, *Works* (1820), IX, 92.

standard — a capacity which can be fructified in art, thought, or action, only by protracted study, broad experience, and continual effort of mind. The development of this capacity is ethical in its aim; "virtue is the highest proof of understanding, and the only solid basis of greatness; and . . . vice is the natural consequence of narrow thoughts."

"A fallible being," he once said, "will fail somewhere"; and it is true that, as a literary critic, Johnson did not always practice what he preached. But to estimate his precepts by his own occasional unfair judgments, as was so often done during the nineteenth century, is to lose sight of the forest for the sake of a few shrubs. One sometimes confronts the charge, moreover, that Johnson often labors the obvious. He intended to do so; for he believed that men in general do not need to be informed so much as they need to be reminded. In as pertinent a statement as was ever made about Johnson, Reynolds once remarked that "he cleared my mind of a great deal of rubbish." And upon almost all occasions Johnson both informed and reminded with a masculine honesty and with an inimitable and trenchant good sense which make him, as Mr. T. S. Eliot has said, "a dangerous person to disagree with." Taine's peevish complaint of him that "his truths are too true" would have been regarded as a compliment by Johnson, who felt that the truth was an important matter and that it would bear repetition.

It has also been urged, during the last century or so, that Johnson was not, in an exact sense, a "critic"; Irving Babbitt, indeed, believed that no Englishman has been one. But it may be questioned whether any humanist — and least of all Babbitt — is distinctively a critic. For the humanist seeks to find a significance in art which transcends technical criticism; he may be said to regard the critic who is not first of all a moralist as falling short of man's primary function; and in this respect, for example, there is perhaps some justification for Adam Smith's famous verdict on Johnson's *Preface to Shakespeare* as "the most manly piece of criticism ever published in any country." Johnson considered himself, certainly, as a moralist: to him, the "laws of criticism" were of little import unless they reflected or subserved those of "nature"; his concern was with the end of art, and he evaluated the means chiefly in proportion as it enabled the conception of the ultimate to become ethically realizable.

Only the adequate comprehension of truth will insure ethical fruition; art has, as its primary purpose, the inculcation of truth; and when Johnson stated that "Books without the knowledge of life are useless; for what should books teach but the art of *living?*" the knowledge of life which he emphasized is the knowledge of universal or, as he called it, "general nature." In addition to the indispensability of this knowledge for ethical development, "nothing can please many, and please long, but just representations of general nature." In the midst of the reverberations in English literature of extreme neo-classic rationalism and of the reactions which appeared in opposition to it, the classical conception of ideal or general nature was most sanely held and best displayed by Dryden, Swift, and Pope, although they also exemplify in microcosm, especially Pope, most of the other current tendencies of their age. The final declaration of this primary classical principle by Johnson and Reynolds was even less trameled by contemporary extremes, and was characterized by a genuine breadth of comprehension.

The function of the artist, especially that of the poet, is a high one: he is to serve, said Johnson, as "the interpreter of Nature and the legislator of mankind," and to preside "over the thoughts and manners of future generations"; and, in order to accomplish this end,

He must divest himself of the prejudices of his age and country; he must consider right and wrong in their abstracted and invariable state; he must disregard present laws and opinions, and rise to general and transcendental truths, which will always be the same.[2]

[2] *Rasselas* (1759), chap. x.

This standard is also the fundamental test by which art is to be evaluated. Since that alone is "general nature" which is unalterably true, distortion or complete falsity in art ensues from the obtrusion of merely individual feelings; from the restricted concentration upon particulars and upon piecemeal or partial aspects; from subservience to the fashions and opinions of a given nation or period; or from any systematization of rules which cannot be demonstrated to have its foundation in the ethical ideal of man's nature. More than any other writer of his century, Johnson opposed such essentially unclassical tendencies with an incorruptible if rugged honesty, with a broad ethical understanding, and with his own perpetual and pervasive common sense — a distinctive combination of qualities which gives him a position to which that of perhaps no figure in any other literature is quite comparable.

"Nothing is good," said Johnson, "but what is consistent with truth and probability." Against the probable may be placed the romantically "marvelous," which, far from necessitating greater invention from the artist, needs very little; "he that forsakes the probable may always find the marvelous"; and

while readers could be procured, the authors were willing to continue it; for when a man had by practice gained some fluency of language, he had no further care than to retire to his closet, let loose his invention, and heat his mind with incredibilities; a book was thus produced without fear of criticism, without the toil of study, without knowledge of nature, or acquaintance with life.[3]

The few patterns by which the "marvelous" is presented, moreover, become quickly stereotyped; and of the many "novels and romances that wit or idleness, vanity or indigence, have pushed into the world, there are very few of which the end cannot be conjectured from the beginning." A taste for the "marvelous" may be propelled merely by restlessness, boredom, or the desire

[3] *Rambler*, No. 4.

to avoid thought; indeed, its vogue in either prose or verse is chiefly as an opiate for "those that are weary of themselves," and who "have recourse to it as a pleasing dream."

Just as a narcotic devotion to the "marvelous" reveals the predominance of subjective impulse over objective insight, the isolated portrayal of the particular, or the overuse of particulars in stylistic illustration, also manifests a limited and subjective preoccupation. The poet "does not number the streaks of the tulip"; to do so is to lose the "grandeur of generality" and its central and idealized significance. Johnson's famous strictures on the "metaphysical poets" are partially based on this assumption; for though he respected their originality and learning, he believed that the force of their metaphors was lost in such scrupulous enumeration as they employed, and that "the mind by the mention of particulars is turned more upon . . . that from which the illustration is drawn, than that to which it is applied." The poets of this school too often "lay on the watch for novelty," and their occasionally "labored particularities" failed to exhibit the sublimity which accompanies the presentation of the wide prospects of general manners and life;

they never attempted that comprehension and expanse of thought which at once fills the whole mind, and of which the first effect is sudden astonishment, and the second rational admiration. Sublimity is produced by aggregation, and littleness by dispersion. Great thoughts are always general, and consist in positions not limited by exceptions, and in descriptions not descending to minuteness. . . . Their attempts were always analytick: they broke every image into fragments. . . .[4]

A further consequence of extreme particularity in style — as in subject — is a risk of obscurity, at least to subsequent generations; and the classical principle that perspicuity is the first obligation of the artist was firmly held by Johnson. A similar danger accrues from "pedantry" and "by pedantry is meant that minute

[4] Johnson, Life of Cowley, *Works*, IX, 19, 45.

knowledge which is derived from particular sciences and studies in opposition to the general notions supplied by a wide survey of life and nature." Thus, Johnson viewed somewhat askance Milton's use of Latin idiom; and he felt that Shakespeare, in some of his declamations or set speeches, was less concerned with inquiring what the occasion prompted than in showing what his extraneous knowledge could supply. Or again, he censured Pope's *Imitations of Horace* as necessitating a specialized information in the reader. Imitations may reveal great industry and close observation; the learned may occasionally be surprised or pleased by an unexpected parallel; but the direction of imitations is particularized and restricted, and "their effect is local and temporary; they appeal not to reason or passion, but to memory, and presuppose an accidental or artificial state of mind. An Imitation of Spenser is nothing to a reader, however acute, by whom Spenser has never been perused." [5]

Similarly, in the portrayal of human nature, an overconcentration on the specific particular not only diverts the gaze from the central and ideal reality to the defective accident, but also, because the particular by itself usually appeals only to changing conditions and interests, it may also fail to affect the reader except momentarily. It seems probable that Johnson, at least in his critical writings if not in conversation, would never have quarreled severely with the best realistic literature of the following century; for, provided he was convinced that such literature did not sanction looseness, he certainly preferred an accurate presentation of empirical or particularized nature to a completely lifeless idealization. He was even fonder of Fielding than he chose to admit in conversation; and though he violently told Hannah More that *Tom Jones* was a "vicious" book for her to read, he forgot to prevent himself, when he praised a character of Fanny Burney's, from enthusiastically saying, "Harry Fielding never drew so good a character! — such a fine varnish of low politeness!" Yet he felt

[5] Johnson, Life of West, *Works,* XI, 263.

that an overconcern with the concrete particular, when once admitted, does not easily stop, and that it may quickly become indiscriminate; like Keats or Hazlitt, for example, he would not have agreed with Wordsworth's sentiments about Old Matthew or Simon Lee.

For Johnson concurred with the traditional tenet of classicism that, except in comic art, the human beings selected for portrayal must at all times be sufficiently endowed to elicit, by a sympathetic credibility, a corresponding feeling and thought in the observer; and he consequently condemned the photographic representation of characters who appear too remote from the ideal: "The noblest beauties of art are those of which the effect is co-extended with rational nature, or at least with the whole circle of polished life; what is less than this can be only . . . the plaything of fashion and the amusement of a day." [6]

He censured the vogue of pastoral writing partly because of its insipidity: "an intelligent reader acquainted with the scenes of real life sickens at the mention of the *crook*, the *pipe*, the *sheep*, and the *kids*, which it is not necessary to bring forward to notice" — subjects which can please only "barbarians in the dawn of literature, and children in the dawn of life." But he felt even more strongly that pastoral characters as a rule had little to offer mentally, unless probability were violated in presenting them: "At the revival of learning in Italy it was soon discovered that a dialogue of imaginary swains might be composed with little difficulty, because the conversation of shepherds excludes profound or refined sentiment." [7]

II

Lack of permanent appeal and of objective truth to general nature also result from a concentration on the customs of a particular age and from a desire to satisfy the opinions which are

[6] *Loc. cit.*
[7] Johnson, Life of Ambrose Philips, *Works*, XI, 252.

conditioned by its social *milieu*. Much of the satire with which the eighteenth century abounds has as its purpose the illustration of the chasm between universal nature and transient social custom. A contrast might be emphasized by presenting a Utopia, as in the land of the Houyhnhnms; or the uncorrupted reactions of an external observer might be noted, as in the first three voyages of Gulliver, or as in the common device of placing in western Europe a bewildered stranger from a remote country. The intention in all such cases, of course, was to jolt the reader's subjective or unthinking acceptance of the manners and beliefs of the specific society in which he is cast. The poet, said Johnson, must write "as a being superior to time and place"; he who does not write thus, "easily finds readers, and quickly loses them." Thus Butler's *Hudibras* recedes further from public notice with every decade; for despite its wit and a certain generality of direction, the folly and hypocrisy it exposed were based upon manners and illustrated by allusions which had significance for little more than the time in which it was written.

Homer, for example, survives because his "positions are general, and his representations natural, with very little dependence on local or temporary customs." Shakespeare is perhaps without equal as a poet of "general nature," as a poet "who holds up to his readers a faithful mirror of manners and of life": his employment of his characters is "not modified by the customs of particular places, unpractised by the rest of the world; by the peculiarities of studies or professions, which can operate but upon small numbers; or by the accidents of transient fashions or temporary opinions." [8] Shakespeare subjected his characters to common occurrences, and then inquired what they would have felt and thought in reaction to these occurrences. The reactions he presents are those of men of all ages; and if, to Rymer, Dennis, and Voltaire, his Romans do not appear sufficiently Roman, or his kings completely kingly, it is because he "always makes nature pre-

[8] Johnson, Preface to Shakespeare, *Works*, II, 80.

dominate over accident." Attacks on Shakespeare's disregard of the changeable "drapery" of local customs and decorums "are the petty cavils of petty minds. A poet overlooks the casual distinction of country and condition, as a painter, satisfied with the figure, neglects the drapery."

But if art is to present rather "the passions of men, which are uniform, than their customs, which are changeable," it should not distort the importance of any one emotion or impulse in order to accord with a fashionable vogue. Thus, the principle of the "ruling passion," which abetted the artificial decorum of rigidly fitting every action or sentiment to a given type of character, was ridiculed by Johnson. Similarly, he cast an unfavorable eye on the rather exorbitant role which, beginning with the Restoration, was given to "romantick love" in the drama, and which, as it was represented there, almost gave the impression that the relation of the sexes was the "ruling passion" of everyone and at every moment. Owing to popular demand and the ease with which the romantic-love drama could be written, this tendency was to become even more strongly entrenched in subsequent periods, with the result that many critics "first endured, then pitied, then embraced"; but it was always energetically combated in English neo-classic criticism; and various uneasy and even amusing attempts were made to fix the guilt. A relatively common explanation of its rise was the growing number of women in the reading public and the theater audience. Elizabeth Montagu, however, insisted that the blame should be attributed to recent French example; and a nationalistic reviewer of her *Essay on Shakespeare* (1769), as well as a few other writers, agreed with her. Critics of the earlier rationalistic school, such as Gildon, had condemned romantic love as without sufficient "dignity" for serious drama; while John Upton, who believed that women were responsible for its literary prevalence, thought it suitable only as a "comic passion." [9] Others censured its new preponderance as

[9] *Critical Observations on Shakespeare* (1746), pp. 15, 32–33.

effeminate and morally enervating: "One of the most remarkable differences betwixt ancient and modern tragedy," declared Joseph Warton, for instance, "arises from the prevailing custom of describing only those distresses which are occasioned by the passion of love . . . which, by totally engrossing the theatre, hath contributed to degrade that noble school of virtue into an academy of effeminacy." [10] Still other critics, in the latter half of the century, objected to its ascendance on historical grounds, and maintained that, since its dominance was of recent origin and confined to western Europe, it could be designated as a gratification of only a transitory and local taste. Johnson's objections were largely moral: he felt that so widespread a devotion to it on the stage would increasingly encourage an opinion, at least among those of lighter minds, that all other propensities and endeavors are and rightfully should be subordinated to it; thus Dryden's *All for Love* "has one fault equal to many, though rather moral than critical, that by admitting the romantick omnipotence of Love, he has recommended as laudable and worthy of imitation that conduct which through all ages the good have censured as vicious." [11] Waller, though he wrote too many "amorous verses," at least "is not always at the last gasp; he does not die of a frown, nor live upon a smile." But the ethical "depravity" of making romantic love "the universal agent . . . , by whose power all good and evil is distributed, and every action quickened or retarded," arises chiefly from its distortion of "general nature." It is characteristic that Shakespeare viewed it as

only one of many passions; and as it has no great influence upon the sum of life, it has little operation in the dramas of a poet who caught his ideas from the living world, and exhibited only what he saw before him. He knew that any other passion, as it was regular or exorbitant, was a cause of happiness or calamity. [12]

[10] *Adventurer,* No. 113.
[11] Johnson, Life of Dryden, *Works,* IX, 334.
[12] Preface to Shakespeare, *Works,* II, 82.

Johnson's broad application of the principle of "general nature" was also characterized by a repudiation, on rational rather than emotional grounds, of many of the neo-classic rules for creating and judging art. "It ought to be the first endeavour of a writer to distinguish nature from custom; or that which is established because it is right, from that which is right only because it is established"; and Johnson also applied the designation of mere "custom" to rules which only "blind reverence" or "arbitrary edicts" had established. His consideration of the rules was in keeping with Pope's injunction that

> Nature, like liberty, is but restrained
> By the same laws which first herself ordained.

The "laws of nature" are superior to all of the "accidental prescriptions of authority." Individual caprice has been responsible for many rules: self-authorized legislators, "out of various means by which the same end may be attained, selected such as happened to occur to their own reflexion," and then sought to give them "the certainty and stability of science."

More frequently, rules have arisen as a specious form of imitation. In a broad sense, imitation is to be commended. Johnson seems to have subscribed to a common contention of the period that the art of the first cultivated age of a nation or a civilization is usually the best. Whether the aesthetic genius of a people be exhausted with its youth, or its attention be turned to other endeavors; or whether, as is more likely, the first writers had so successfully represented the most probable occurrences and the most striking aspects of human nature that little is left for succeeding generations except to transpose the same incidents and recombine the same images, "it is commonly observed that the early writers are in possession of Nature, and their followers of art; that the first excel in strength and invention, and the latter in elegance and refinement." The approach to the general truth of nature, in many of the works of the ancients, has been tested by the repeated judgment of centuries; and since nature is constant, some imitation of the general and ultimate effects of such works is almost inevitable if the artist sincerely attempts to portray the essential and the lasting; for his study of nature must be aided and verified by the general principles of works which have been long examined and approved. But to imitate the particular characteristics of a writer is to "tread a beaten walk"; and in this respect, "no man ever yet became great by imitation."

Indeed, Johnson repeatedly emphasized that the ancients are great partly because their sentiments and descriptions were derived from their own direct study of nature; and when Edward Young's *Conjectures on Original Composition* (1759) appeared, he concluded that Young had studied literature with little thought, or he would not have urged as novelties what, in many instances, should be taken for granted as common maxims. To imitate the ancients in accidental and particular respects rather than in their fundamental motive and ideal is as much a neglect of "general nature" as is submission to the arbitrary codification of rules expounded by the school of Rymer and echoed in "the minute and slender criticism of Voltaire." It was in this spirit, for example, that Johnson wrote his famous defense of Shakespeare's neglect of artificial decorums in the presentation of character, and supported his disregard of the unities of time and place and of the rule which forbade the intermingling of tragedy and comedy. Indeed, at least in conversation, Johnson could easily be brought to maintain that, though neither had much to defend it, even individual predilection was preferable to an exclusive and narrow obedience to rule. He told Fanny Burney that, among the judges of her work,

the first are those who know no rules, but pronounce entirely from their natural taste and feelings; the second are those who know and judge by rules; and the third are those who know, and are above the rules. These last are those you should wish to satisfy. Next to them rate the natural judges; but ever despise those opinions that are formed by the rules.[13]

Except for his insistence on the unity of action and on such decorums as he believed absolutely necessary for general probability and for ethical instruction of some sort, the only specific rules which Johnson much stressed were the classical and in some cases neo-classic rules of vocabulary, metaphor, and versification; and those of his strictures on which the nineteenth century most frowned were in general only stylistic in their purpose.

IV

Against the unchanging universal, both human ethics and art are to be judged. To make the individual man "the measure of all things" is ultimately to sanction the impressions of individual sensibility. The optimistic confidence of the followers of Shaftesbury in the direction and validity of one's own sensibility, upon which both romantic relativism and the nineteenth-century belief in progress were in part to rest, was as little shared by Johnson as it would have been by any classical humanist; nor would he have agreed with a recent authoress who, writing about Shelley, maintained that "Christ was the first romantic, and the greatest." In his insistence that ethical fruition necessitates rational insight, Johnson, like Swift, continually faced and distrusted the evil and fluctuation inherent in animal nature and the empirical world. In the *Tour to the Hebrides,* Boswell relates that Lady McLeod, who was something of a "benevolist," inquired whether man's feelings were not of themselves directed generally to the good. Johnson replied, "No, Madam, no more than a wolf." "Lady McLeod," said Boswell, "started at this, saying in a low voice, 'This is worse than Swift.'" Johnson, indeed, was in agreement with the Hobbists that actions or inclinations which are helpful to others and appear virtuous are, when prompted by feelings, ultimately initiated by self-interest,

[13] *Diary and Letters of Madame D'Arblay* (ed. Dobson, 1904), I, 183–184.

vanity, uneasiness, or occasionally, depending upon external circumstances, by a momentary good-humor; he radically differed from them, however, by maintaining the possibility of a rational conception of the good. Though we hardly need take the statement seriously, we may at least remember the amusing and perhaps suggestive definition of a romantic as one who does not believe in original sin and the fall of man. Mrs. Chapone, in talking with Johnson, "wondered to hear a man, who by his actions shews so much benevolence, maintain that the human heart is naturally malevolent, and that all the benevolence we see in the few who are good is acquired by reason and religion." [14]

To Johnson, Shaftesbury's statement that atheism is the product of "ill-humor" was only too applicable to the ethics of all the "benevolists"; for virtue based on temperament was certain to be as feeble and unreliable as its foundation. He would have agreed with Swift that its resolutions would hardly "last till the next morning, or rather to the next meal." When Boswell was feeling well disposed, and was also elated by an unusually fine spell of weather, he once happily exclaimed that he wished "to be benevolent to all mankind." Johnson "looked at me," he reported,

with a benignant indulgence; but took occasion to give me wise and salutary caution. "Do not, Sir, accustom yourself to trust to *impressions*. . . . By trusting to impressions, a man may gradually come to yield to them, so as not to be a free agent, or what is the same thing in effect, to *suppose* that he is not a free agent. . . . There can be no confidence in him, no more than in a tyger." [15]

In his plea for literary originality, Edward Young stated that "An original may be said to be of a vegetable nature. . . . It grows, it is not made." Johnson would have readily acquiesced in this; but he would also have regarded the complete "original" as being rather remote from the ideal nature of man, and would have sanctioned Goethe's remark that we get little from our own entirely

[14] Life of Mrs. Chapone (1807), prefixed to her *Works* (Boston: 1809), I, 56.
[15] Boswell, *Life of Johnson* (June 3, 1781).

native feelings but stupidity and awkwardness. "The mental disease of the present generation," Johnson stated, "is impatience of study, contempt of the great masters of ancient wisdom, and a disposition to rely wholly upon unassisted genius and natural sagacity." Such a statement is not inconsistent with Johnson's censure of the servile imitation of the particular modes of representation which the ancients employed. Reason is eternally the same; the structure of a plot or a given variety of images need not and should not be. In its disregard of objective reason and of the fixed standard of the ideally good, the "original" sentiment of the individual, far from being "free," is tied by its very character to the subjective and the changing: it is elicited and determined by that which is immediately before it; and if it does manage to transcend the floating desires of the individual ego, its attention becomes directed by the desires and opinions, hardly less subjective, narrow, and transitory, of the immediate society about it. "That which is to be loved long," said Johnson, "must be loved with reason rather than passion"; "the mind can only repose on the stability of truth"; and, in both their aesthetic and moral ramifications, freedom and self-fruition can accrue only from a total and rational grasp of the immutable ideal.

Johnson's conception of the nature of rational insight is not easy to define with precision. It is certain only that he regarded it as a far more complete exertion of mind than mathematical abstraction, and that he would not have agreed with some of the extreme neo-classic rationalists, especially those on the continent, that sheer method or logic can attain insight. That he felt no need himself to analyze the cognitive and judging process may indicate that he took for granted the customary broad classical conception of it. To the Greeks, the faculty (*nous*) for conceiving the universal and ideal was distinguished from the capacity (*sophrosyne*) to utilize experience in practical "good sense" or judgment; but humanistic wisdom necessarily embraced both. The same distinction may be observed in Latin; but there the conception of practical wisdom (*sapientia*) is far more comprehensive and may be said to include, in its complete function, the insight (*ratio*) into the ideal. It is probable that Johnson, whose own mind was somewhat more Latin in character than Greek, conceived of reason and judgment generally as approaching most closely to *sapientia*, in its highest connotation. For though he considered that reason, like nature, is "uniform and inflexible," and that its proper sphere is not the fluctuatingly tangible but the unchanging ideal, he also ruggedly maintained that, in the all-important matter of practical conduct and judgment, an empirical use of wide experience and of the study of the experience of others is a necessary accompaniment. The arguments of neither the severe rationalists nor of the supporters of an instinctive and unaided "inner sense" removed Johnson, in the slightest degree, from this rather characteristically English confidence in the practically known.

In the employment of experience, however, every attempt must be made to lift it from the fashionable and local. "Whatever withdraws us from the power of our senses, whatever makes the past, the distant, or the future predominate over the present, advances us in the dignity of thinking beings." Such a breadth cannot be achieved without the study and application of the practical experiences of the past as shown in the history, not of political events, but of manners and of values. "To judge rightly of the present, we must oppose it to the past; for all judgment is comparative. . . ." Biographies of men in various periods and localities are especially to be esteemed "as giving us what comes near to ourselves, what we can turn to use." The concrete reactions of the past to aesthetic as well as moral endeavors and principles are at all times to be consulted. Mathematical demonstration has little to fear from the experience of man; but the greatness of the *Iliad* as an "imitation" of general truth — though it also necessitates insight into the ideal — can hardly be estimated, in comparison with other works, except by the concrete examples of its practical substantiation in the approval of succeeding generations; for no "imitation" is absolute, but only "comparative." "Of the first building that was raised, it might be with certainty determined that it was round or square; but whether it was spacious and lofty must have been referred to time." To works, therefore,

of which the excellence is not absolute and definite, but gradual and comparative; to works not raised upon principles demonstrative and scientific, but appealing wholly to observation and experience, no other test can be applied than length of duration and continuance of esteem.[16]

V

Aesthetic judgment, then, should ideally involve a conception of "general nature," which is achieved and retained by a total and consequently ethical realization of mind; and, with this conception as its standard, it estimates the truth and propriety of a work of art as an "imitation" of that ideal. As such, it is, in the broadest sense, essentially a rational process which conceives the ideal and which, in so far as it evaluates aesthetic or ethical "imitations" in comparison with each other, naturally draws upon experience and a wide study of the experience of others. But both the creation and understanding of art must also include the use of the passions and the imagination. The nature and working of the passions of man are among the primary subjects of art; and passion can hardly be presented or understood without some susceptibility to it. Again, "the end of poetry is to instruct by pleasing"; and Johnson, unlike some of the severer rationalists, continually emphasized the classical precept of using the passions to inculcate truth. He added only the qualification that restraint, through the imposition of the decorum of the ideal, was obligatory in employing them; for he would have agreed with Goethe that "anything that emancipates the spirit, without a corresponding growth in control, is dangerous." Johnson's attitude towards "novelty," for example, reflects this standpoint: he repeatedly emphasized its importance in art and considered aesthetic pleasure to be almost impossible without it; but he carefully distinguished between "to please" and "to divert." The desire

[16] Preface to Shakespeare, *Works*, II, 78.

for novelty in and for itself is purely emotional: it arises from restlessness or from "the common satiety of life"; and if it is once allowed to be an end in itself, it will grow by what it feeds on, and only licentiousness and falsity to nature can result.

Johnson's conception of the function of the imagination was in a similar vein. One of the *Ramblers* dealt with "The Luxury of Vain Imagination," and one of the chapters of *Rasselas* with "The Dangerous Prevalence of Imagination." But his often-cited distrust of the imagination was primarily ethical; what he distrusted was only the danger of its complete and untutored preponderance in the mind — a state which, after all, is not far from insanity; for long-continued and extreme illusion, he thought, may easily become delusion. If a completely uncontrolled imagination turns on its possessor, he must, said Johnson with rare common sense, inevitably "conceive himself what he is not; for who is pleased with what he is?"; and if, without rational direction, it turns outward, it will perceive little more than what individual fears or desires prompt. Again, rooted as it ultimately is in sense-impressions, it tends to concentrate too exclusively on the empirically fluctuating, and can never by itself alone rise to the permanent and ideal.

Such a standpoint was no more than a continuation of the neo-stoic and indeed of the general classical distrust of the imagination and the passions as controlling guides of moral action; but it was partly accentuated in Johnson himself by a fear of his own vivid imagination and active feelings, and by an almost compensatory attempt to restrain them. Indeed, Johnson's reassertion of many principles was characterized by a continual and honest struggle with his own inclinations in order to attain a consistent purpose and a clarity of judgment. Thus, he was prey to an extraordinary and almost pathological indolence. Yet, in his essays, he condemned few vices so sternly — and with so much acumen and understanding — as idleness; with violent outbursts of energy, he sought to overcome it; his posthumously published *Prayers and Meditations* are full of pathetic resolutions to counteract it; "surely," he would write, "I shall not spend my whole life with my own total disapprobation." He was as prone to melancholy as was Swift, and his severity with Swift was partly owing to his own fear of surrendering to despondency, his belief that Swift had done this, and his conviction that "despair is criminal." Instances of such conflicts within himself, of both greater and less importance, abound in Johnson. Sir Joshua Reynolds, who knew him so well, considered an awareness of them as indispensable to any understanding of Johnson: "Were I to write the Life of Dr. Johnson," he said, "I would labour this point, to separate his conduct that proceeded from his passions, and what proceeded from his reason, from his natural disposition seen in his quiet hours."

Indeed, it is partly owing to such struggles with himself that there is so often a ring of conviction in the statements of this heroic figure: his pervasive and humane common sense bears a stamp of both honesty and authority because he himself had known and felt the apprehensions and temptations which he sought to dispel. And even when he wrote, for example, that "life is a state in which much is to be endured, and little to be enjoyed," this statement, simple as it is, was not the idle precept of an observer but a reflection wrung from the experience of a more than usually active and courageous participant in the vicissitudes of life. Similarly, imaginative literature had a strong emotional effect on Johnson; the reader of *Macbeth*, he stated, "looks around alarmed, and starts to find himself alone." Johnson "would inveigh against devotional poetry," wrote Mrs. Piozzi, "and protest that all religious verses were cold and feeble"; yet when he would try, for example, to repeat the *Dies irae, Dies illa*, "he could never pass the stanza ending thus, *Tantus labor non sit cassus*, without bursting into a flood of tears." He was even "immoderately fond of reading romances of chivalry," according to Bishop Percy, and would partly "attribute to their extravagant fictions" an "unsettled turn of mind" which disturbed him. Against "that hunger of imagination which preys incessantly upon life," as against many other tendencies in himself, Johnson assiduously strove; and his diary bears witness to his apprehensive resolves, with every year "to reclaim imagination."

But although, reinforced by the conflicts of his own inclinations, he reiterated the classical distrust of the imagination as a practical moral guide, he consistently — as did other contemporary moralists when they turned to art itself — took it for granted that the imagination was not only indispensable in any valid aesthetic creation or reaction but that it had a very important place in "genius" applied in any direction. When Pope had written

> But not in Fancy's maze he wander'd long,
> But stoop'd to truth, and moraliz'd his song,

he implied not that the entire realm of the imagination was a "maze" but that he had rejected that part of it which was one. Similarly, Johnson's disapprobation was directed to "The Luxury of a *Vain* Imagination," to an imagination which was not "informed" and "regulated" by reality; and when he stated, in a too often quoted sentence, that he had tried to allot few papers of the *Rambler* to "the idle sports of imagination," the inference is not that the imagination has only "idle sports" to offer but rather that he had attempted to avoid those "sports" of it which *were* idle. The more imagination one has, the better, if it is counterbalanced in equal degree with knowledge and rational control.

Indeed, "it is ridiculous to oppose judgment to imagination; for it does not appear that men have necessarily less of the one as they have more of the other." The happiest function of the imagination necessitates the accompaniment of guidance and control, just as complete judgment itself is impossible without the presence and participation of a fertile and gifted imagination. For since the imagination and the passions naturally tend to respond to what is immediately and individually felt, it is the task of reason, in any estimation of conduct or of a work of art, to make sure that what is immediately present is not the haphazard product of chance or fashion. The task of reason, in short, is to hold to the ideal and the true with such firmness and clarity as to give an *immediacy* to truth; and this immediacy, if sufficiently vital, will almost automatically elicit, persuade, and then school and direct imaginative and emotional response. This traditional precept of classicism, with its corollary that art should "instruct by pleasing," — that it should, in other words, draw upon and then inculcate the emotions with the standard and decorum of the ideal, — is therefore assumed by Johnson; and such a standpoint is by no means to be confused with the almost total anti-imaginative and anti-emotional bias of Cartesian mathematicism or of extreme neo-classic rationalism generally.

VI

The presidential *Discourses* which Sir Joshua Reynolds delivered before the Royal Academy (1769–1790), though they were pedagogical and hence restricted in their purpose, were comprehensive in their ultimate directions and conclusions. Owing partly to the length of time over which they were given, partly to the increasing influence of Johnson, and partly to Reynolds's own open-mindedness, many critical tenets are present in these addresses which had elsewhere been supported only separately; and when taken together, Reynolds's *Discourses* comprise perhaps the most representative single embodiment in English of eighteenth-century aesthetic principles. But throughout all of his *Discourses* Reynolds declared as his primary standpoint the humanistic conception of ideal nature; and his increasing admission, under the heading of ideal nature, of elements that were perhaps not strictly classical, is indicative of an ability for reconciliation and compromise which is distinctively characteristic of much English criticism.

The end of art, Reynolds maintained, is ethical enlargement: virtue is to be acquired only by a firm grasp of the immutable ideal of man. In attaining this end, art, in accordance with classical tradition, may first of all neglect the non-human world, or view it as merely complementary to man: the portrayal of animal life or of landscape may often draw a just applause for manifesting technical skill, or sensitivity to line, color, and proportion; but it may not claim the highest praise. Again, in the depiction of human beings, art strives to "imitate" the ideal by exhibiting an ultimate and completed model. Reynolds, in this respect, is genuinely classical; and the reflections on painting and sculpture which he occasionally cites from classical writers are in the spirit he himself has adopted. The deformities or peculiarities which a strict verisimilitude to the particular would show are to be viewed as "deficiencies" in imitating the ideal. Although Alexander the Great, for instance, was of short stature, and St. Paul of "mean" appearance, the great painters of the Italian Renaissance did not represent them thus: these painters attempted, rather, to present the character of their subject by approximating its appearance to the ideal — external appearance being all that a painter has as his medium — and then essayed to "show the man by showing his *action*." The Dutch realistic painters, in their fidelity to the particular, have occasionally been called "true to nature": but "particularities cannot be nature; for how can that be the nature of man, in which no two individuals are the same?"

With only visual materials at their disposal, "imitation" by painting or sculpture of the ideal nature of man must, as in classical antiquity, include the presentation of a finished figure, which only the fullest physical development, in every respect, could have formed. Particular development is of various kinds; but the disclosure of ideal nature, as far as visual means can accomplish it, is not to be found

in the Hercules, nor in the Gladiator, nor in the Apollo; but in that form which is taken from all, and which partakes equally of the activity of the Gladiator, of the delicacy of the Apollo, and of the muscular strength of the Hercules. . . . It cannot consist in any one to the exclusion of the rest: no one, therefore, must be predominant, that no one may be deficient.[17]

[17] Discourse III, *Discourses* (ed. Johnson, 1891), p. 89.

Since the accentuation of particular features or aspects detracts from the unity of the completed result, personal expression in the subject has no place in the highest art. If expression is admitted, however, every attempt must be made to generalize it, and to declare it by means of the *action* of the total figure rather than by the more individual means of facial aspect. Thus, although

the Laocoön and his two sons have more expression in the countenance than perhaps any other antique statues, yet it is only the general expression of pain; and this passion is still more strongly expressed by the writhing and contortion of the body than by the features.[18]

The disclosure by the artist of the total capacity of the human figure, necessitating as it does that every individual expression or feature be subdued to a general consonance, will thus embody the temperate decorum of the ideal. Hamlet's advice to the players, said Reynolds, is to be taken to heart by the painter: "the purpose of playing" is at all times to hold "the mirror up to nature"; yet "in the very torrent, tempest, and — as I may say — whirlwind of passion, you must acquire and beget a temperance, that may give it smoothness."

But although Reynolds repeated the classical contention that the visual arts should represent the *ethos*, or the fixed and universal character, rather than the *pathos*, or feeling, which is fluctuating and individual, his later discourses betray a deep-seated if not too articulate conviction — a conviction which is not severely classical — that the highest art should perhaps possess a union of the two; and it is characteristic that he should have increasingly dwelt upon the example of Michelangelo, whose works display a preëminent and perhaps unparalleled coalescence of both tendencies. Eighteenth-century critics, who were fond of antitheses, often opposed Michelangelo and Raphael, as they did Homer and Virgil, or Dryden and Pope: until the latter quarter of the century, preference was usually given to Raphael; and although the proficiency of Michelangelo in drawing and design was always regarded as

[18] Discourse X, p. 248.

unequaled, his later figures were often condemned as "extravagant" in their tension and energy. As early as one of the papers
which he wrote for the *Idler* (1759), however, Reynolds advocated the study of Michelangelo as "the Homer of painting," and
added that "One may safely recommend a little more enthusiasm
to the modern painters; too much is certainly not the vice of the
present age." Reynolds maintained that, although he occasionally
"transgressed the limits" of classical decorum, Michelangelo's
works are in "the sublimest style" of painting; and this standpoint
also reveals a characteristic reconciliation, on Reynolds's part, of
two diverse conceptions of sublimity.

The "sublime," as it was presented and urged in English criticism of the first half of the eighteenth century, may be said to have
been equated more often than not with the universal, the *beau
ideal*. The separation of the beautiful and the sublime, and the
analysis of sublimity on the basis of associationist principles as a
somewhat subjective reaction, were encouraged by such works as
John Baillie's *Essay on the Sublime* (1747) and Edmund Burke's
Sublime and Beautiful (1757), and later became extremely common. Reynolds may thus be said to have approached, with more
genuineness than most of his contemporaries, the spirit of Longinus:
he inclined neither to the completely decorous idealization of one
extreme, nor to the associational emotionalism of the other. His
concern was with the ideal, and, like Johnson, he regarded sublimity as the accompaniment of the "grandeur of generality."

But Reynolds increasingly maintained the importance of the
Longinian state of transport in the grasping of it: he came to urge
that only when such a vigor as is found in Michelangelo accentu-
ates, sustains, and makes it immediate, in a total realization, can
the sublimity of the ideal be best known and felt; and he believed
that, in order to achieve in either aesthetic execution or understanding such a power, vigor, and total immediacy of ideal representation, a vital but directed employment is necessary of *pathos* or
feeling. Thus, in his fifth discourse (1772), Reynolds felt com-

pelled by conscience to tell his pupils that "our judgment must, upon the whole, decide in favor of Raffaelle"; for Raphael possessed a larger number of esssential attributes, not least among them a continual awareness of the strict decorum of the ideal. But Reynolds could not help adding the qualification that, if the sublime is the highest excellence in art, and if it atones for any deficiencies, the decision must be against Raphael; indeed, he even permitted himself to admit that though Raphael "had more taste and fancy," Michelangelo "had more genius and imagination."

In his last discourse (1790), Reynolds openly maintained that the sublime *is* the highest end of art, that the sublimity of the ideal is best typified by the works of Michelangelo, and that, in comparison with his achievement in rendering the ideal immediate and vital, "the little elegancies of art . . . lose all their value." Painting and sculpture have been "in a gradual state of decline from the age of Michel Angelo to the present"; and if the "lost taste" for the genuinely sublime disclosure and comprehension of the ideal is to be recovered, youthful artists must study the figures of Michelangelo as assiduously and sympathetically as he himself did the works of the Greeks. With the modesty and the sincere generosity which always characterized him, Reynolds frankly disclaimed his own work, and concluded by stating that, if he had anything to recommend himself, it was that he could

appear in the train, I cannot say of [Michelangelo's] imitators, but of his admirers. I have taken another course, one more suited to my abilities, and to the taste of the times in which I live. Yet however unequal I feel myself to that attempt, were I now to begin the world again, I would tread in the steps of that great master . . . to catch the slightest of his perfections would be glory and distinction enough for an ambitious man.

. . . and I should desire that the last words which I should pronounce in this Academy, and from this place, might be the name of MICHEL ANGELO.[19]

[19] Discourse XV, pp. 372–373.

The word "taste," in early English neo-classic criticism, had been commonly applied to only an untutored and innate sentiment: with this application, it often served as a keynote to the critics of the *je ne sais quoi* faith and to the Shaftesburyan "benevolists," while to other writers, who regarded aesthetic evaluation as involving reason and experience, the word was in general little used simply because of its restricted connotation. By the middle of the eighteenth century, however, the term was frequently employed in almost every sense, even by the same critics and reviewers. A writer for the *World* (1753) despondently concluded, for example, that "no idea at all" could be attached to "the poor monosyllable TASTE." Largely because of this confusion, it rapidly became applied, more often than not, to almost any aesthetic reaction — "to that act of mind," as Reynolds said, "by which we like or dislike, whatever be the subject"; and consequently, all that could be said to enter into this reaction was potentially connoted by the word. As "taste" is now employed in general usage, continued Reynolds,

Our judgment upon an airy nothing, a fancy which has no foundation, is called by the same name which we give to our determination concerning those truths which refer to the most general and most unalterable principles of human nature: to the works which are only to be produced by the greatest efforts of the human understanding.[20]

"We are obliged to take words as we find them," he added; the matter is not largely one of language, therefore; if taste be used in place of approval, preference, or evaluation, the problem is still to discover what is excellent and valid in art, and what is necessary for the conception of that excellence.

VII

Taste or preference in its crudest form, Reynolds had stated in one of the *Idlers,* is the result of a joint pleasure in novelty and excitement and in the evoking of associations which are either

[20] Discourse VII, pp. 177–178.

personal or else imbibed from immediate and accidental social custom; and the temporary and unschooled pleasure from such a reaction leads many people mistakenly to attribute "beauty" to the cause which elicits it. But taste, in its valid and objective sense, is a total employment of mind. Truth of whatever sort is the ultimate aim and province of the intellect generally; and, in art, truth may result from the agreement and propriety with themselves of these primary and essential ideas or ideals which are employed and depicted as the subjects of art; from the agreement of an "imitation" with its original; or, lastly, "from the correspondence of the several parts of any arrangement with each other." Taste is "good" or "bad" in proportion to its capacity to gauge the extent and quality of this truth; it is, in short, the "power of distinguishing right from wrong" in the arts; and the right, the true, which is "unalterable and fixed" and which constitutes the "standard of taste," is

that presiding principle of . . . the general idea of nature. The beginning, the middle, and the end of everything that is valuable in taste, is comprised in the knowledge of what is truly nature; for whatever notions are not conformable to those of nature . . . must be considered as more or less capricious.[21]

Thus, the first requisite in forming a completely "just taste" is to have recourse to "reason and philosophy." It is occasionally objected that the intrusion of philosophy in taste restrains the imagination and induces an overscrupulousness which borders on timidity; but "Fear is neither reason nor philosophy. The true spirit of philosophy, by giving knowledge, gives a manly confidence, and substitutes rational firmness in place of vain presumption"; and if any production of art disdain or shrink from this just "rational firmness," it will be that of the idly fanciful or impulsive, and certainly not the manly and "exalted enthusiasm of a sound and true genius."

The primary principle of taste, which is the imitation of nature,

[21] Discourse VII, pp. 180–181.

is thus immutable; and "with regard to real truth . . . the taste which conforms to it is, and must be, uniform," without consideration to individual opinions or transitory social customs and predilections. Yet, in the empirical world, there are "opinions and prejudices" which have a kind of temporary validity, application, or cause; such phenomena, "which may be called truth upon sufferance, or truth by courtesy, . . . [are] not fixed but variable"; and that aspect of taste which may judge the satisfaction or fulfillment of them may be allowed to be variable in the same proportion. While these "opinions and prejudices" continue, they operate with most people as a form of truth; and consequently, the empirical or "secondary" capacity of taste may be indulged to some extent. The indulgence must be discriminatory: "as these prejudices become more narrow, more local, more transitory, this secondary taste becomes more and more fantastical"; and it is thus an imperative function of good sense and historical study to attempt, in the presentation and comprehension of empirical and fluctuating truth, to select only those opinions which are sanctioned in other cultivated ages and societies as well as one's own, and which "on account of their duration and extent, . . . become capable of no small degree of stability." The general temper of "what has pleased, and continues to please, is likely to please again"; and in proportion "as these prejudices are known to be generally diffused, or long received, the taste which conforms to them approaches nearer to certainty, and to a sort of resemblance to real science, even where opinions are found to be no better than prejudices." [22]

The effort to determine what can generally please is especially facilitated by the study of major works, esteem of which has transgressed the limits of a given period or society; and through them, "the accumulated experience of mankind may at once be acquired." A knowledge of several arts should be had as well; the painter ought, in particular, to be conversant with the poets; for many aesthetic principles can be discovered or at least fully realized only

[22] Discourse VII, p. 179.

through an awareness of the distinctive analogies which one art bears to another. Further, at least some acquaintance must be presumed with "the nature and internal fabric and organization, as I may call it, of the human mind and imagination," and also with the difference between the character and working of associations which are subjective and local and those which have always or usually been general to cultivated mankind. But although a catering to empirical opinions and subjects be permissible and indeed necessary in eliciting or reinforcing emotional interest and pleasure, they must always be used — as Michelangelo, in particular, used them — in such a way as will not violate but, if possible, even assist in rendering immediately the primary aim, which is the conception of ideal nature.

Genuine taste, then, which is impossible to achieve without — in their widest implication — "reason" and "good sense," is a full exertion of mind which perceives the ideal, and which at the same time estimates, in relative proportion to other works of art, the extent and success with which the ideal is communicated in a given production. The strength and comprehensiveness of this grasp of mind are augmented and directed, not only by the study of the mind itself, of the general principles of art, and of the history of taste, but also by extensive experience with the character and potentialities of specific mediums of art, and by the generalizations which have been made with the aid of that experience. The rules of art, at their best, constitute the generalizations of the past experience of mankind with particular aesthetic mediums. The pedagogical obligations imposed on Reynolds, in counseling younger artists as the President of the Royal Academy, led him in his earlier discourses to stress rules more strongly, perhaps, than he would otherwise have done; and, as the specific rules which Johnson emphasized were generally stylistic, those which Reynolds urged were largely technical. Others, such as the concern of art with the ideal, the necessity of a subject being of "general interest," the stress on action rather than expression, were broadly classical injunctions.

Further, when Reynolds exhorted the technical imitation of the great artists of the past, he was not advocating "the borrowing of a particular thought, an action, attitude, or figure, and transplanting it into your own work" — a species of imitation which is "confined, illiberal, unscientific." He was counseling only a study of purpose, manner, and technique, and an early application of them in order to inculcate and render intrinsic the fruits of that study; and such imitation as this has traditionally characterized the youth of any great artist. Reynolds cited Raphael, for example, who began by imitating completely Pietro Perugino, and who then progressed to a more liberal imitation of the drawing of Michelangelo; he learned coloring from Leonardo, moreover; and to this, he added the study of all the ancient remains in Italy, and hired other men to draw for him what could be found in Greece.

The beauty of natural and unschooled inclination is extolled almost as little by Reynolds as by any other classicist. He who relies, at least in his formative years, "on his own sense, has ended his studies as soon as he has begun them." Early imitation of past excellence, as a formative guide, is a fetter only to the weakly impulsive. Even the most highly endowed talent "cannot subsist on its own stock"; and it is characteristic that Michelangelo and Raphael neglected no opportunity to make themselves "possessed of all the knowledge in the art which had been discovered in the works of their predecessors." The complete "original," whose primary concern is self-expression, can have little self which warrants expression, or at least which justifies the attention of succeeding generations; and, far from being able to boast of himself as unimitative, he "will soon be reduced, from mere barrenness, to the poorest of all imitations; he will be obliged to imitate himself."

Reynolds would have agreed with Goethe that "a subjective nature has soon talked out his little internal material, and is at last ruined by mannerism"; and that "desire and need for intercourse with great predecessors is a sure sign of a superior ability." If latent talent exists, selective imitation and industry will improve it, by infusing the principles and spirit of "those noble works that ought always to be present in our thoughts"; and, if talent is lacking, at least a few absurdities and total misrepresentations will be avoided. Rules of themselves are not oppressive evils; they become so only when formulated and preached by the unimaginative and the impotent, whose "frigid minds" mistake the particular and unessential detail for the general purpose and method of the man. The young artist who should journey to Italy,

and spend his whole time there only in copying pictures, and measuring statues or buildings (though these things are not to be neglected), would return with little improvement. He that imitates the Iliad, says Dr. Young, is not imitating Homer. It is not by laying up in the memory the particular details of any of the great works of art, that any man becomes a great artist, if he stops without making himself master of the general principles on which these works are conducted.[23]

The aid this broad study offers is in "forming a *mind*, adapted and adequate to all times and all occasions," a mind which, having "appropriated" these principles and techniques into itself, may then execute and judge with increasing independence of the details of former works. Further, such general principles are helpful only as they contribute to the ultimate goal "of seeing nature." They cannot be so employed without a constant mental grasp, reference, and application of fundamental purposes — of the aim and character, in other words, of humanistic art; and without this application, Reynolds shrewdly remarked, "A provision of endless apparatus, a bustle of infinite inquiry and research, or even the mere mechanical labour of copying, may be employed to evade and shuffle off real labour — the real labour of thinking."[24]

VIII

The function of the educated and disciplined taste is not to be regarded as a series of isolated and dispassionate deliberations on

[23] Discourse XI, p. 276.
[24] Discourse XII, p. 283.

the basis of experience and knowledge; its action is single and immediate, and the ideas and principles which it employs are "digested," and are then retained, as it were, in potential effect. Reynolds, who gave a unified expression to so many of the English critical tendencies of his age, substantiated this conviction by one of the general conclusions of contemporary associationist psychology. The mind may be determined and molded by the character of what it contemplates; it adapts itself to that character; it takes on, as by infection, the attributes which it discerns — it expands in conceiving the sublime, contracts in noting the minute, and becomes lax in attending to the disordered. The mind is easily and quickly narrowed by associations which arise from one's contiguity to what is locally and transitorily practiced and esteemed; and, as in every form of lasting intellectual endeavor, the attempt must be made in art to employ this associative process to advantage rather than be controlled by its coöperation with chance and fashion.

Reynolds therefore implied that the decline of art since the high Renaissance may be in part attributed to a growing predominance of the fashionable and momentary in the associations of both artist and spectator. By the sympathetic and acute study of artists whose works have stood the test of the ages, we may "catch something of their way of thinking"; ideas which before "lay in embryo, feeble, ill-shaped, and confused," may thus be developed, consolidated, and directed; but at all times "we must not content ourselves with merely admiring and relishing, we must enter into the principles on which the work is wrought." By means of the prolonged contact which is established through "the habit of contemplating and brooding" over the works of such artists, the principles and conceptions to which the observer is exposed will eventually become "a part of himself," and be "woven into his mind"; he will "pass over whatever is commonplace and insipid"; he will in time find it impossible, at least, "to think or invent in a mean manner; a state of mind is acquired that receives those ideas only which relish of grandeur and simplicity."

The contemporary tendency to use "reason" as synonymous with "theoretical deliberation," and with the abstractly logical, ultimately led Reynolds, in one of his last discourses (1786), to consider the word inapplicable to this absorptive, total, and immediate function of mind; he wished to stress that knowledge genuinely affects taste, not as material for discursive consultation, so to speak, but only when it becomes inextricably interwoven with the entire texture of mental and emotional response; and his late declaration that the final appeal of the arts is to the "imagination" indicates the increasing scope which this term was beginning to possess. The imagination, neglecting "principles falsely called rational," is in art the ultimate "residence of truth": it is a kind of "sagacity" which is, in the true and comprehensive sense, "right reason"; it supersedes "the slow progress of deduction, [and] goes at once, by what appears a kind of intuition, to the conclusion." Within this intuition is the accumulated response to a firm, rational grasp of the ideal, to study and experience, and to "very many and very intricate considerations" which are too numerous and subtle to avail separately in logical deduction but which, joined together thus, act as an instinctive touchstone; and this intuitional result of thought, study, and of "the accumulated experience of our whole life . . . ought to prevail over that reason, which, however powerfully exerted on any particular occasion, will probably comprehend but a partial view of the subject."

Reynolds may be said to have felt that the restriction of "reason" had somewhat mirrored itself in the art and taste of his day; in his old age, he condemned his own work as an illustration of it; and he came to oppose this restriction in art almost as much as he did the reliance on uninformed and independent sentiment, impulse, or fashion. But his final selection of "imagination" rather than "reason" as a term to suggest the principal receptacle, as it were, of taste was largely owing to the exigencies of contemporary vocabulary. For, like Johnson, he never wavered from his conviction that the true province of art is to imitate the objective and unchanging truth of "general nature," and to shape in accordance with this truth the ethical character of man; and, somewhat more than Johnson, he combined with this conviction a belief that imitation of the ideal can be effectively presented and realized only if it is rendered vital, impressive, and emotionally immediate.

It is significant that, as embodied in the writing of these two men, the last major assertion in English of the classical principle of "general nature" was not only one of the most energetic but at the same time one of the sanest and most inclusive. For the premises of English neo-classicism found in Reynolds their most broadly representative expression and in Johnson their most triumphantly humane application.

CHAPTER IV.

THE GROWTH OF INDIVIDUALISM: THE PREMISE OF THE ASSOCIATION OF IDEAS

The conception of the existence and validity of the universal or ideal, with a consequently unalterable standard of taste as its corollary, is one of the great legacies of Greek humanistic thought. A relativistic and pragmatic approach, which tends to rest upon a confidence in the particular alone, is occasionally revealed, of course, in classical thought from the Sophists through the Epicureans, and was by no means completely absent during the Middle Ages; but it hardly began to be exploited in European thought until the advent, in the seventeenth century, of Baconian experimentalism and especially of British empirical psychology.

A previous chapter mentioned the extent to which British experimental empiricism, in its earlier stages, joined with and helped to augment the anti-emotional and anti-imaginative bias of extreme neo-classic rationalism generally. Yet its direction is almost diametrically opposed to that of classicism: to the empiricist, knowledge comes wholly from sensation, or from reflection upon that sensation; insofar as we actually reason at all, therefore, "we reason," said Locke, "about particulars"; and for insight into the objectively general, empiricism substitutes the mere term "generalization," with its connotation of a subjective act of mind. In its opposition to the universal, and in its emphasis upon sensory and experiential proof, it is also essentially anti-rationalistic: it turns in distrust upon the generalizations which the "meddling intellect" is prone to make for the sake of convenience; in the reasoning process itself, as in other phenomena, it accepts that alone which constant and direct experience can verify; and, if carried far enough, its extreme results may easily become a skeptical relativism, and a final inability to rely upon much more than individual sentiment.

The aesthetic and critical reverberations of these tendencies of British empiricism become pronounced and then extend widely throughout western Europe by the latter half of the eighteenth century; and, in doing so, they form the groundwork for the somewhat heterogeneous body of assumptions, inclinations, and values which is called romanticism. For European romanticism, as it emerged historically, may perhaps be most generally defined as a turning away, in whatever direction, from the classical standard of ideal nature, and from the accompanying conviction that the full exercise of ethical reason may grasp that objective ideal. In more or less degree, it substitutes for these premises the beliefs that such truth as can be known is to be found primarily in or through the particular, and that this truth is to be realized, appreciated, and declared in art by the response to that particular of some faculty or capacity in man which is imaginative and often emotional rather than "rational," and which therefore inclines to be somewhat individualistic and subjective in its working. It is for this reason that romanticism branches into so many different directions, and that no one specific work of art, no one purpose, mood, interest, or *genre,* is in any sense completely typical of it.

The English transition to empirical aesthetic criticism was not, of course, abrupt. Many neo-classic tenets, in varying degree, survived in the works of almost all the later eighteenth-century critics; some even persisted well into the following century; and a few, particularly those which had to do with prose exposition, have never since been totally disregarded. But if we except the writings of Dr. Johnson, of Reynolds, and of a few others, most of the enormous body of British criticism in the second half of the eighteenth century is increasingly particularized, and tends to fall very roughly under the headings of stylistic and psychological analysis.

Before this period, for example, neo-classic discussions of rhetoric had been rather general: now, however, problems of diction, meta-phor, sentence-structure, and prose-rhythm were investigated in great detail, with continual reference to concrete illustrations. This half-century also witnessed the flowering of the study of English versification. Few problems in English prosody have since been discussed which were not explored or at least recognized then. In addition to prosodic analyses on more or less orthodox grounds, the famous "bar and rest" school of English metrists, after a few false starts by less ingenious writers, was ushered in by Joshua Steele, who thought that most five-feet iambic lines had really either six or eight feet. In order to prove this and other rather startling assertions, he formulated an elaborate and never fully understood system of musical symbols to illustrate the pitch and timbre of the speaking voice, the potentialities of which he considered similar to those of the drone of a bagpipe; and although he soon abandoned versifica-tion for philanthropic work in the West Indies, his results were reiterated, combated, or reapplied by a fair number of other metrists with the same general ambitions. Not only professed prosodists and rhetoricians, but also general critics and even a few historians, philosophers, clergymen, and physicians embarked upon empirical analyses of versification and prose-style; and most of these writers gave careful attention to the particular auditory effects — as shown by specific examples or deduced from them — of stress, pause, balance, assonance, and the like.

A still larger portion of the empirical criticism of this period was concerned with the psychological nature of aesthetic creation and response. Even titles are indicative, such as that of James Beattie's *Essays on Poetry and Music, as They Affect the Mind* (1776). We may recall, moreover, the rather sudden cult in the eighteenth century of the uneducated and "original genius," which in its cruder form gave small and fitful vogue to figures like Stephen Duck, "the thresher poet," and the blind Thomas Blacklock, and which contributed to the popularity of Robert Burns; and an interest in the precise nature and working of genius is continually apparent in contemporary criticism, and the bases for most of the popular nineteenth-century English discussions of genius were generally established there. Few philosophical and critical works, moreover, lack discussions in some detail of "taste," — by which was generally meant, especially in the last quarter of the eighteenth century, all that enters into aesthetic judgment, inclination, and preference; and the concern, in such discussions, was why or at least how the human mind is led, by the distinctive character of its own constitution, to react to art as it does.

The psychological criticism of this period was either determined or, more often, strongly colored by the doctrine of "the association of ideas"; it may be questioned, indeed, whether any philosophical or psychological doctrine has since permeated critical thought in so great a degree as did that of the association of ideas at this time. Associationism, in its simplest and most general sense, implies only that ideas which are similar or which have repeatedly occurred simultaneously or in succession tend automatically to evoke one another. Thus, by repeated experience, the perception of a *cause* may lead us to think of or look for an *effect*. By *resemblance*, moreover, a picture recalls the thought of its original. Or a plant, as one writer stated, may suggest an image to a poet, for example, and its species to a botanist: "it operates on the imaginations of both, by *resemblance;* on the poet, by the resemblance of its general appearance, or of some of its particular qualities, to a distant subject; on the botanist, by the exact resemblance of its parts to individuals of the same kind." [1] Or association may work by *contiguity* in time or place: the odor of an apple may suggest the color and shape of it; the idea of a given place will recall the idea of another seen next to it or near it; or the thought of one event will elicit the thought of another which followed or preceded it. In addition to cause and effect, resemblance, and contiguity, other

[1] Alexander Gerard, "Of the Influence of Habit on Association," *Essay on Genius* (1774), pp. 138–139.

less basic principles of mental connection may be cited. That of contrariety would be one, for example: thus, as in *Henry IV*,

a monarch groaning under the cares of government, and kept awake by his disquietude, will readily think on the ease of the peasant, and reflect,

> How many thousand of my poorest subjects
> Are at this hour asleep!

The reflection is suggested by a twofold contrariety, that between the meanness of the subject and the elevation of the king, and that between the ease of the former and the restlessness of the latter.[2]

II

The tendency of British associationism, as it developed during the eighteenth century, was to view the entire mental and emotional nature of man as a bundle of habits which have been formed on the basis of these principles. The rapidity with which associationism influenced aesthetics may not only be attributed to a general state of mind which welcomed a satisfying empirical explanation for aesthetics; it was partly owing to the traditional literary character of British philosophy in general, especially in the latter half of the eighteenth century. Few philosophers of the period, when they sought to illustrate mental processes, failed to discuss the arts; and the relationship between critics and philosophers — especially in Scotland, from which the bulk of contemporary criticism emanated — was very close.

Thomas Hobbes, in his avowed attempt to prove that knowledge arises from sensation alone, had earlier directed renewed attention to the natural sequences into which ideas tend to fall. Locke, who originated the phrase "association of ideas," shortly afterwards emphasized the importance of "attention," of "repetition," and of "the accompaniment of pleasure and pain" in fixing ideas in the memory; he distinguished between a "natural" corre-

[2] Gerard, "Of the Qualities of Ideas Which Produce Association," *Essay on Genius*, p. 113.

spondence in ideas and a connection established by "chance" or "custom," and he regarded it as one of the proper functions of judgment to make such a distinction in every circumstance. The immediate influence of Locke on early eighteenth-century criticism is best exemplified in Joseph Addison. Subscribing as he did to Locke's conviction that knowledge is a fitting together of what is congruous and a separation of what is incongruous in the ideas which experience supplies, Addison consequently considered that, by holding firm to the knowledge which is thus empirically achieved, habit and custom may in time transfer and mold the inclinations to it, and thus develop aesthetic taste or indeed any sort of judgment. We have only, as Pythagoras said, to

"Pitch upon that course of life which is the most excellent, and custom will render it the most delightful. . . ." The voice of reason is more to be regarded than the bent of any present inclination, since, by the rule above-mentioned, inclination will at length come over to reason, though we can never force reason to comply with inclination.[3]

But, as his papers on taste and the imagination reveal (*Spectator*, Nos. 409, 411–421), Addison's very assumption of an empirical position forced him to base his conception of taste as much upon subjective reactions as upon a just comprehension of objective nature. According to Locke, it will be remembered, only density, extension, figure, and motion may be designated as "primary" qualities of matter; all other qualities cannot be proved to be anything else than the result of the mind's own subjective working. By admitting, with Locke, the individual activity of the mind in receiving and combining "primary" ideas and in virtually creating ideas which are "secondary," Addison, at least in theory, was led to sanction, as one of the tests of a work of art, its ability to "please" simply by evoking this activity. Thus, the imitation, which art strives to render of its object, provokes an "action of mind which compares the ideas arising from the original objects with the

[3] *Spectator*, No. 447.

ideas we receive from the statue, picture, description, or sound, that represents them." The evoking of this "action of mind" not only accounts for much of the pleasure of art,

but makes us delight in all the actions and arts of mimicry. It is this that makes the several kinds of wit pleasant, which consists . . . in the affinity of ideas: and we may add, it is this also that raises the little satisfaction we sometimes find in the different sorts of false wit; whether it consists in the affinity of letters, as an anagram, acrostic; or of syllables, as in doggerel rhymes, echoes; or of words, as in puns, quibbles . . . [4]

Addison, therefore, regarded not only "beauty," which diffuses a "satisfaction and complacency through the imagination," as an aesthetic quality; but, since imaginative activity in the comparison of ideas is a fundamental exertion of taste, the use of "novelty" and "surprise," which help to call forth this activity, is to some extent necessary in art; and the "new or uncommon," within limits, is thus a valid aesthetic means. In addition, "greatness" — by which Addison implied "sublimity" — is also as legitimate a qualification for art as is beauty. Locke's sensationalist psychology had encouraged the belief that the greater the size of the object contemplated or recalled, the greater is the feeling or thought which results. By the view, said Addison, of "a vast uncultivated desert, of huge heaps of mountains, high rocks and precipices, or a wide expanse of waters," the imagination is "flung into a pleasing astonishment"; for "The mind of man naturally hates everything that looks like a restraint upon it, and is apt to fancy itself under a sort of confinement, when the sight is pent up in a narrow compass. . . . On the contrary, a spacious horizon is an image of liberty. . . ." [5]

"Greatness," in other words, by challenging the capacity of the mind and the emotions, frees them for their fullest possible exercise. This general attitude, like Addison's conception of the effect of imitation, is indicative of a gradual tendency which encouraged

[4] *Spectator*, No. 416.
[5] *Spectator*, No. 412.

the romantic stress on subjective "suggestiveness" in art as an end in itself — a "suggestiveness" which gives pleasure by the very action it forced the imagination to undergo. For with the complete skepticism of immutable reason and ideal nature in which empirical psychology was fast culminating, the extorting of a subjective activity in comparing and combining ideas became not merely a conscious aim but one of the fundamental purposes for the very existence of art.

Between Locke and the close of the eighteenth century, British associationism tends roughly to evolve in two directions. In the first place, there is a more extreme tendency to regard the mind as being totally derived from association. It is usually frankly utilitarian in its moral assumptions: man pursues pleasure, and seeks to avoid pain; the association of certain ideas with pleasure and pain forms habits of thought or feeling which result in principles, incentives, and actions. Associationism, as an all-inclusive basis for psychology and ethics, was first ably though briefly urged by John Gay (1731), who was a cousin of the poet with the same name. Gay's thesis was expanded and systematized in a work entitled *Observations on Man* (1749) by David Hartley, whose influence on romantic poetry of half a century later is well known, and for whom Coleridge, in a burst of enthusiasm, even named his first son. To Hartley, association completely governs both the mind and emotions. Its physiological counterpart is the action of the nervous system upon sensations: when an object is sensed, vibrations or "tremblings" carry its impression through the "white medullary substance" of the nerves and spine to the brain, where they coalesce into a unified conception. Man starts, then, as a collection of "vibratiuncles": he is "a kind of barrel-organ," as one writer has stated, "set in motion by the external forces of the world." [6] But through association, man develops step by step; activities, impressions, and thoughts become habitual and automatic; and they are combined and coalesced into more complex and refined impulses

[6] Sir Leslie Stephen, *English Thought in the Eighteenth Century* (1927), II, 64.

and conceptions. Primitive and crude instincts may thus eventually attain ideal expression; egotism may at last flower forth in disinterested benevolence and even fervent universal sympathy. In addition to having other immediate followers, Hartley was developed and popularized by two characteristically versatile Englishmen: by Joseph Priestley, who was the discoverer of oxygen, a theologian, a writer on political subjects, and also a literary critic; and by Erasmus Darwin, who was a physician, a naturalist, a philosopher, and a poet, and who, by applying the hypothesis of associational evolution to biological instincts as well, helped to prepare the way for the doctrine advanced by his famous grandson.

A second major tendency of British associationism, less extreme and dominant than the former, may be discovered in the use made of it by the large body of writers who comprised the eighteenth-century portion of the Scottish "Common-Sense School" of philosophy and criticism. Scottish philosophy had quickly warmed to the Shaftesburyan conception of the innate "moral sense"; this very emphasis upon subjective or at least emotional reaction had stimulated an empirical analysis of it; and a combination of the doctrine of moral sentiment with that of associationism, in the first half of the eighteenth century, is found in such Scots as Francis Hutcheson and George Turnbull, and, somewhat later, Adam Smith.

With its greater stress upon innate intuitions, the Scottish school sought to avoid both the extreme materialism of some of the English associationists and the complete skepticism which Hume had shown to be the logical end of empiricism generally, and it assumed a position of sturdy compromise which is very British. Especially under Thomas Reid and somewhat under Dugald Stewart, it therefore opposed excessive analysis. Despite whatever conclusions may result from metaphysical speculation, it regarded the existence of both matter and the soul as beyond quibble and as intuitionally self-evident. The mind is not formed exclusively by the repetition of experience and association, although they are admittedly necessary: it is innately endowed with a valid capacity to receive, employ, and guide what experience brings. The Scottish school thus extended the reach and scope of direct intuition to a common-sense acceptance of matter of fact. In its combination of an intuitionalism, which includes both sentiment and common sense, with a conservative use of empirical associationism, the Scottish philosophy represents a distinctive compromise and fusion of almost all of whatever eighteenth-century British tendencies of thought cannot be described as classical or humanistic — although, in very British fashion, it also occasionally reflects values and attitudes which are far from unclassical.

III

The concern of this chapter, however, is not to give a résumé of the history of British associationism, or to instance the successive contributions of its specific proponents; the intention is simply to stress those general conclusions or tendencies which were employed and developed by contemporary English aesthetics, and which later served as the main foundation for many of the familiar tenets of English romantic poets and critics. As Hume had said, it is always possible to urge that "a thousand different sentiments, excited by the same object, are all right; because no sentiment represents what is really in the object"; and that "Beauty is no quality in things themselves: it exists merely in the mind which contemplates them; and each mind perceives a different beauty." The general empirical emphasis on individual and subjective reaction to art received a heartening encouragement from British associationism. It is characteristic that the Scottish associationist, Archibald Alison, in his popular *Essays on Taste* (1790), should have devoted the first half of his book to discussing "The Nature of the *Emotions* of Sublimity and Beauty," and to analyzing "The Exercise of the Imagination," and only afterwards have turned to "The Sublimity and Beauty of the Material World."

The more extreme associational position may be typified by

Abraham Tucker's statement that "nothing is beautiful in itself"; that beauty is essentially a general feeling of satisfaction and interest which accrues when the working of man's associational capacity is evoked in a certain way or combination of ways. One of such appeals, said Tucker, may be made by means of "order"; and "objects stand in order when their situation corresponds with that of our ideas." The associational principles of contiguity or cause and effect, for example, become so ingrained in the mind by natural aptitude and by habit that when an arrangement of objects is such as to appeal to those principles, the arrangement may be grasped with firmness, quickness, and totality, and is thus designated as "order." A second means by which beauty may be felt — provided it does not fundamentally violate order — is "succession," or "variety," the value of which arises in helping to keep the mind in play and thus prevent monotony. Tucker designated a third source of beauty as "translation," or "transference": when ideas or objects have been associated, from experience or natural inclination, with a feeling of pleasure, the pleasure is transferred, by association, to the idea or object itself, and is identified with it. A fourth, which is in some respects the "most plentiful source of beauty," and which employs associational transference as well, is "expression": that which reveals what we conceive to be the genuine character of a particular is a cause of delight. In proportion as it exhibits actions or sentiments which we esteem as morally good, the mere expression also gains in beauty; for we transfer the pleasure and confidence felt in the presence of the good to the expression itself.

The contention here that beauty is what pleases by according with the associational construction of the individual mind is also implied in more moderate associationist criticism; and since the determining factors vary greatly among individuals — in the strength and sensitivity, that is, of inherent capacity, and in the controlling associations to which chance environment has exposed one — the result, which is "beauty," would appear to be equally relative. Yet, unless all evaluation is to be abandoned, a certain standard of taste is necessary. Indeed, a standard of sorts may surely be assumed, wrote Edmund Burke; "for if there were not some principles of judgment as well as of sentiment common to all mankind, no hold could possibly be taken either on their reason or their passions, sufficient to maintain the ordinary correspondence of life." [7] A primary step in determining this standard is to distinguish, of course, between those associations which are generally common to cultivated mankind and those which arise from local custom or from restricted, accidental circumstance; and such distinctions were commonly made in associationist criticism.

With the gradual evaporation of the classical conception of the immutable and rationally-conceived ideal, and with the increasing tendency to regard art as a distinctive product of man's mental and emotional nature, characteristic attempts were often made, for example, to arrive at a redefinition of what constitutes the most basic and general appeal of beauty to man's associational capacity; and a widespread theorizing about the essential beauty of form is indicative. The concern of such attempts cannot, as with classical humanism, be said to be the nature of the ethically good, and the manner in which form can assist in rendering the good realizable and humanly pertinent, but rather the intrinsic ability of form as such, whether within or without the pale of ethical value, to elicit associational response. Whatever its end, art is continually characterized by form, whether it be the form of the general structure of a poem, a musical composition, or a painting; whether it be the form of a subdivision of that structure; or whether it be observed, even, in the forms of each of the individual sounds, shapes, or other particulars which are isolated elements in the larger patterns of structure. In the forms exhibited and declared in all works of art — and almost in proportion as they have been able to appeal beyond the moment — certain qualities may be

---

[7] Edmund Burke, "Introduction: on Taste," *Philosophical Inquiry into the Origin of Our Ideas of the Sublime and Beautiful* (1757), *Works* (1792), I, 69.

found in common; and although some difference of opinion existed, among associationist critics, about what these basic general qualities are, they all agreed among themselves and with other contemporary critics upon the indispensability of a just admixture of "uniformity" and "variety."

The delight in such manifestations of uniformity as proportion, order, and regularity — though this pleasure depends upon association — is inherent in all minds, in greater or less degree. Yet perfect uniformity is intolerable to the human mind; and a delight in variety is also inherent. Variety, as Lord Kames stated, should be distinguished from "novelty": variety is impossible without the presence of several particulars or aspects, whereas novelty may arise merely

from a circumstance found in a single object. Again, where objects, whether coexistent or in succession, are sufficiently diversified, the pleasure of variety is complete, though every single object of the train be familiar. But the pleasure of novelty, directly opposed to familiarity, requires no diversification.[8]

Thus, in music, regularity tends to predominate in the rhythm and to some extent in the relations of sounds which comprise a chord, and variety is mainly supplied by the introduction of melody; while a larger use of uniformity and variety may be revealed in the repetition and diversification of themes and later of movements. Form, in art, may almost be gauged by the reconciliation of these two inherent and "natural" principles of beauty. "Nothing is more delightful," said Archibald Alison, "than in any subject where we at first perceived only confusion, to find regularity gradually emerging, and to discover amid the apparent chaos, some uniform principle which reconciles the whole." Indeed, "the pleasure which the mind derives from the perception of similitude in dissimilitude," as Wordsworth later echoed, is not only the basis of art, but is in general "the great spring of the activity of our minds and their chief feeder."

[8] Henry Home, Lord Kames, *Elements of Criticism* (Edinburgh: 1762), I, 329.

The associationists' attempt to discover, by empirical methods, the most essential and, as they conceived, the most strictly classical beauty of form led to a considerable interest in the potentialities of uniformity and variety in elementary poetic images and analogies, in simple sounds, or in primary colors. A characteristic offshoot of this interest was directed to the significance of lines and of simple visual forms, and is thus at least superficially analogous to the intention of some twentieth-century experiments in the visual arts. In his *Analysis of Beauty, Written with a View of Fixing the Fluctuating Ideas of Taste* (1753) — the very title of which indicates the empirical endeavor to arrive at an essential standard — William Hogarth had advanced, as his famous "line of beauty," a serpentine or winding line, the potentialities of which in sculpture and painting he discussed and urged in appreciable detail: it soon became something of a byword in English aesthetics, and was a favorite illustration of many Scottish writers who were interested in associationism. In addition to the combination of uniformity and variety which a winding line may exhibit, it is a "natural" tendency of the mind, as Alison stated, to associate such a line with a subjective but universally desired feeling of "volition and ease": a visual form cannot consist of a single straight line; such a form must be circumscribed, and hence be either angular, curved, or a union of both. The greater part, however, of

those bodies in Nature which possess Hardness, Strength, or Durability, are distinguished by angular Forms. The greater part of those bodies, on the contrary, which possess Weakness, Fragility, or Delicacy, are distinguished by winding or curvilinear Forms. . . . It is also to be observed that from the Sense of Touch angular Forms are expressive to us of Roughness, Sharpness, Hardness; winding Forms, on the contrary, of Softness, Smoothness, Delicacy, and Fineness, and this connection is so permanent, that we immediately infer the existence of these qualities when the bodies are only perceived by the Eye.[9]

[9] Archibald Alison, "Of the Natural Sublimity and Beauty of Forms," *Essays on the Nature and Principles of Taste* (Edinburgh: 1790), pp. 233–234.

A similar interest may be observed in geometrical forms, and earnest but often amusing discussions of such matters as the relative beauty of circles, squares, triangles, and other shapes are not uncommon. Lord Kames, who would have agreed that "Euclid alone has looked on beauty bare," and who felt that variety might be overdone, thought a square, because of its uniformity and simplicity, more beautiful than a hexagon or an octagon. But other critics of the associationist group, like Alison, took issue with such severity, and were more sympathetic with variety; and they might well have claimed authority from Hogarth, who considered an oval, because of the added variety, more beautiful than a circle, and an oval with one end tapered like a cone as more beautiful still. Upon these principles, indeed, Hogarth himself had concluded that the shape of the pineapple was almost the *ne plus ultra* in simple yet varied form, and had cited, as an example of Sir Christopher Wren's "judicious" taste, the use of pineapples as ornaments on the western towers of St. Paul's Cathedral.

From the "natural" associational pleasure in the interplay of variety with uniformity, proportion, and regularity, there arises the aesthetic gratification in conceiving "order," "design," or "fitness." Yet, as soon as simple forms are combined into more intricate ones, a certain relativity, as some associationists recognized, at once ensues: any sort of design presupposes a working towards a given end; and judgment of that design necessitates the perception of its end, and the extent to which the significance of that end is admitted and appreciated. "*Intrinsic* beauty," said Lord Kames, "is discovered in a single object viewed apart without relation to any other object," whereas "*relative* beauty" is

founded on the relation of objects. The former is a perception of sense merely. . . . The latter is accompanied with an act of understanding and reflection; for of a fine instrument or engine, we perceive not the relative beauty, until we be made acquainted with its use and destination. In a word, intrinsic beauty is ultimate; relative beauty is that of means relating to some good end or purpose.[10]

[10] Kames, *Elements of Criticism*, I, 244–245.

"Wherever we discover Fitness or Utility," added Alison,

we infer the existence of Design. In those Forms, accordingly, which are distinguished by such qualities, the discovery of an end immediately suggests to us the belief of Intention or Design; and the same material qualities of Form which signify to us this Fitness or Usefulness are the Signs to us also of the Design or Thought which produced them.[11]

The dependence of any conception of the beauty of design upon a knowledge of its purpose and its end applies not only to what are customarily thought of as works of art; this dependence, with the attendant relativity of aesthetic pleasure, may be especially illustrated by the tendency to discover beauty in

the Forms of Furniture, of Machines, and of Instruments in the different Arts. . . . "A ship which is well built, and which promises to sail well," says Mr. Hogarth, "is called by sailors a beauty." In every other profession in like manner, all Machines or Instruments are called beautiful by the Artists, which are well adapted to the end of their Arts.[12]

IV

Since all beauty, then, becomes relative as soon as simple forms are combined and employed towards a given end, there is an increasing tendency in associationist criticism to agree with Hume that any exertion of taste must first of all presuppose a constant imaginative grasp of the end desired and sufficient knowledge and experience to be acquainted with the merits of the various means by which an end may be achieved; and that, when extensive agreement can be found among arbiters so endowed, "the joint verdict of such . . . is the true standard of taste and beauty." This agreement can be considered extensive only if it transcends the barriers of a specific age. Even more than the conception of what constitutes beauty in its most essential form, the general principles of what is "natural" in the manners and actions

[11] Alison, "Of the Relative Beauty of Forms," *Essays on the Nature and Principles of Taste*, p. 301.
[12] *Ibid.*, p. 340.

delineated, and in the decorums which are to be founded on them, must be largely derived from the analysis of works which have continued to appeal throughout the ages, and from a constant association with them.

Empirical criticism, as a whole, thus found itself in the same position to which the saner Shaftesburyan "emotionalists" — such as James Arbuckle and William Melmoth — had arrived: some external means of reference is necessary to insure agreement; and if rational insight into the ideal is not to be had, and if man's response to art is determined only by subjective sensibility or by the accumulation of experience, no external method of reference is available except the verdict of time. Systems of theology, philosophy, and science, Hume had stated, successively give way to others; but the same is not true of art:

Just expressions of passion and nature are sure, after a little time, to gain public applause, which they maintain forever. Aristotle, and Plato, and Epicurus, and Descartes, may successively yield to each other: but Terence and Virgil maintain a universal, undisputed empire over the minds of men. The abstract philosophy of Cicero has lost its credit: the vehemence of his oratory is still the object of our admiration.[13]

Among writers whose empiricism is not pushed to an extreme, there is an even stronger tendency to regard the verdict of time as "universal" in its application and "founded on nature," and as therefore a revelation of a fixed standard of taste. Though difference of opinion, said Hugh Blair, exists among individuals because of the difference in experience and knowledge and in innate sensibility and strength of imagination, the general character and manner of working in the basic reactions which make up taste are much the same in all people:

Let men declaim as much as they please concerning the caprice and the uncertainty of taste, it is found, by experience, that there are beauties, which, if they be displayed in a proper light, have power to com-

[13] David Hume, "Of the Standard of Taste" (1757), *Philosophical Works* (Boston: 1854), III, 267.

mand lasting and general admiration. In every composition, what interests the imagination and touches the heart, pleases all ages and
nations. . . .

Hence the universal testimony which the most improved nations of
the earth have conspired, throughout a long tract of ages, to give to
some few works of genius; such as the Iliad of Homer, and the Aeneid
of Virgil. Hence the authority which such works have acquired, as
standards in some degree of poetical composition; since from them we
are enabled to collect what the sense of mankind is concerning those
beauties which give them the highest pleasure, and which therefore
poetry ought to exhibit. Authority or prejudice may, in one age or
country, give a temporary reputation . . . [yet] "Time overthrows
the illusions of opinion, but establishes the decisions of nature." [14]

Similarly, to a far greater degree than the rigorous neo-classic
rationalists of the late seventeenth and early eighteenth century,
critics who were influenced by associationist doctrines continually emphasized, as did Johnson and Reynolds, the more liberal
authority of history — although it is to be remembered that Johnson and Reynolds urged the use of this authority as an assistance
and as a contributing substantiation to the rational and ethical
grasp of general nature.

v

But if British associationism ultimately encouraged a certain
subjective relativism of taste, it exerted a far stronger immediate
influence on criticism by its emphasis on the particular, and by
illustrating the existence of an instinctive capacity to incorporate
and guide the ideas which the experience of the particular achieves.
Art, like any other exertion of mind, must essentially attain and
portray its insight through the direct experience of the specifically
concrete, to which alone, said Priestley, "are the strongest sensations annexed"; and he and other writers of the period often

---

[14] Hugh Blair, *Lectures on Rhetoric and Belles-Lettres* (1783), I, Lect. 1.

cited the styles of Shakespeare and the Bible as relying upon the particular. Much of English poetry since the Restoration, thought Hugh Blair, is to be condemned for failing to "particularize the object"; for "we can conceive nothing clear in the abstract; all distinct ideas are formed upon the particular." Yet nothing is more characteristic of British thought as a whole than its simultaneous confidence, not only in the empirically concrete, but also in an almost intuitional absorption of the experience of concrete phenomena, and in the exclusive working of that intuition through the empirically known; and this peculiarly British linkage of empiricism and intuitionalism is especially apparent in many of the primary critical tenets of the later eighteenth century.

It has been mentioned that the connotation of "reason" had been gradually confined in neo-classicism until the word often became synonymous with "abstraction" and consecutive logic. "On the IMMEDIATE," as Coleridge later paraphrased from Schelling, ". . . all the *certainty* of our knowledge depends"; and immediacy of conception arises, not from the "external" and roundabout process of abstraction, but from a continual grasp of the tangible and specific. Yet the particular is meaningless without the molding and coördinating instinct of association: indeed all thought and even habit itself are impossible without this intuitional capacity and direction. And just as it shapes and unifies empirical data, instinctive association is itself developed, informed, and guided by its experience with them. To take the simplest examples:

Even appetite as given by nature [stated one writer], is no more than a pleasing or irksome feeling according to the several degrees of its intenseness. . . . One may observe that little children, when uneasy through hunger . . ., do not know what is the matter with them, and are so far from being moved by appetite towards the gratification of it, that they fight against their victuals and other methods of relief.[15]

[15] Abraham Tucker, *Light of Nature Pursued* (1768–1778), II, 18.

Or again: nothing is more instinctive, said Priestley, than

the endeavour of all animals to recover the *equilibrium* of their bodies, when they are in danger of falling; and yet . . . children have it not, but acquire it gradually and slowly: The same is the case of the action of *sucking*, and the motion of the *eyelids* when anything approaches the eye.[16]

For instinct feeds, as it were, upon experience: the associationists often attempt to show that, although it becomes almost voluntary at the beginning of its application of new experience, instinct of whatever sort ends by digesting experience into itself, until instinct and experience together form a single intuitional touchstone, performance, or cognition. Thus the fruits of all past experience, as Hume had earlier pointed out, are not present as so many "ideas" to be "drawn out," one by one: they exist, rather, as a perpetual "readiness" or "power" of associative response or, as Hume occasionally termed it, of the "imagination"; and, as such, their continual influence, by means of which the imagination is nourished and matured, insures a constant breadth of insight.

Although, as in the later discourses of Reynolds, there is apparent in much of the criticism of this period a general feeling, if not a conviction, that the word "reason" had become too restricted to apply to judgments or reactions which draw upon combined associational intuitions, yet, simply because of the traditional connection of "imagination" with direct sensory experience — which alone was appearing reliable to most empirical thought — this term was at least available for use. Thus Hume had maintained that immediate responses and evaluations cannot be called "reason, which is slow in its operations," and which "is in every age and period of human life extremely liable to error and mistake. It is more conformable to the ordinary wisdom of nature to secure so necessary an act of mind, by some instinct or mechanical tendency . . ."; and he at times, therefore, vaguely at-

[16] In his ed. of Hartley's *Theory of the Human Mind* (1775), Introd., p. xxxi.

tributed immediate and habitual reaction simply to a general susceptibility to "custom," and at other times to the "imagination." There is certainly no intention to imply here that, to most of the associationists or even to the critics influenced by them, the term "imagination" was applicable — as it later somewhat became for many romantic critics — to almost the entire associational capacity of the mind, when it is employed in any non-abstract endeavor. In the works of such Scots as Lord Kames, John Ogilvie, Hugh Blair, and James Beattie, where so many empirical tendencies appear side by side with neo-classic terms and occasionally with an urging of manifest neo-classic values, words such as "reason," "judgment," "imagination," and "taste" are all generally applied, in casual statements, to specific and therefore limited faculties; and the same is true of critics who were even more swayed by associationist doctrines. As a consequence, there are often superficial oppositions, such as that of "judgment" with "imagination," which occasionally retained its restricted classical connotation of an "image-making" faculty.

The differentiation of "taste" and "imagination" is particularly superficial and casual: taste will be said to include imagination, for example; and yet imagination will be considered incomplete without taste. But when the word "imagination" is employed in a comprehensive sense, it is usually understood to apply to a rather vague combination of innate sensibility, the power of association, and the faculty of conception — a combination which is peculiarly susceptible to habit, and which therefore matures with experience and exercise. On the other hand, a close examination of the vocabulary of these writers reveals that the same combination is also more or less assumed as necessary for "taste" or even "judgment," in their highest and most valid capacity, or indeed for almost any comprehensive action of mind whatsoever.

It is therefore characteristic that the various works devoted exclusively to the question of taste, such as those of Alexander Gerard, Archibald Alison, or Richard Payne Knight, should attempt an analysis of man's entire mental and emotional working, as it is directed to art and the subjects of art, and that in doing so they should especially emphasize the imagination. Any really extensive investigation of taste, in short, tended to follow the example offered by Edmund Burke, whose primary purpose was to discover the means by which "the imagination is affected"; for

to cut off all pretence for cavilling, I mean by the word Taste no more than that faculty or those faculties of the mind, which are affected with, or which form a judgment of, the works of the imagination and the elegant arts. That is, I think, the most general idea of that word. . . . And my point in this inquiry is, to find whether there are any principles, on which the imagination is affected . . . as to supply the means of reasoning satisfactorily about them.[17]

It may be generally said, indeed, that, as it is applied to active creation or invention in art, and often in other operations of mind as well, the union of innate sensibility, of experience and knowledge, and of man's total associational response was increasingly connoted by the word "imagination"; and that when it applies to a somewhat more passive and more strictly judicial capacity — a capacity in which knowledge and experience are even more emphasized — its function was usually designated as "taste."

Among a few writers, moreover, like Alexander Gerard, there is even a tendency to regard the working of the imagination as analogous if not actually identical with the ability of instinctive association generally to absorb all experience into itself. The imagination serves as the groundwork for almost all mental exertions: it "forms the embryo," said one writer, "of everything which originates from human intellect"; it gives to abstraction, judgment, or invention, for example, acumen and significance in any relatively isolated and limited functions of their own. Hume had intimated as much in stating that "the memory, senses, and understanding are . . . all of them founded on the imagination."

[17] Edmund Burke, "Introduction: On Taste," *Philosophical Inquiry into the Origin of Our Ideas of the Sublime and Beautiful* (1757), *Works* (1792), I, 71.

But in addition to serving as the basis or at least as an indispensable element in any of the individual aspects of mind, the imagination ultimately fructifies and emerges as a process combining them all.

This general attitude is especially apparent in Abraham Tucker, whose *Light of Nature Pursued* (1768–1778) was abridged and edited by William Hazlitt (1807), and whose psychology, as it applies to aesthetics, permeates most of Hazlitt's literary criticism, and, indirectly through Hazlitt, apparently had some influence on Keats. To Tucker, all "instinct" of whatever sort, "falls under the class of imagination"; in fact, he often implies that almost every aspect of mind must ultimately fall under the connotation of that "general term." We may perhaps make a rough distinction, he stated, between "whatever knowledge we receive from sensation, or fall upon by experience, or grow into by habit," and that knowledge which "has been infused into us by careful instruction or worked out by . . . industry": the former may be designated as the direct "produce of the imagination," while the latter, achieved through conscious effort, "may be stiled the attainments of the understanding." Yet the understanding, in this sense, is still only a refined and specifically directed aspect of mind which "grows out of the imagination." "The understanding," Hume had once said, as distinct from the "trivial suggestions of the *fancy*," may almost be defined as "the general and more established properties of the imagination." But as the knowledge thus consciously won becomes absorbed and automatically applied, the judgments of the understanding are appropriated, Tucker added into "the property of the imagination." Indeed, there is "no more reason to suppose one faculty for apprehending, another for judging, and another for reasoning, than to suppose one faculty for seeing blue, another for yellow, and another for scarlet." [18]

[18] Abraham Tucker, *Light of Nature Pursued*, I, 330, 338–339, 351–353, and *passim*.

Some foreshadowing may thus be observed, in Tucker, of the not uncommon romantic conception of the imagination as almost comprising the use, with unusual intensity and instinctive facility, of the total unconscious mind. As this conception became more prevalent at the close of the century, other terms accordingly came to denote more limited and partial functions of the mind. "Fancy," as used by some Scottish writers who anticipate Coleridge's distinction between "fancy" and "imagination," became gradually such a term, and was applied to a particular combinatory and "aggregative" capacity of association. Such words as "abstraction" or "judgment" tended to connote a *conscious* use of specific aspects or potentialities of mind with a deliberate end in view. But any such deliberate or refined exercise of thought relies, said Tucker, upon that entire store of "assemblages, associations, trains, and judgment . . . [which] together with the repository containing them we stile the *Imagination*." Similarly, whatever is gained from such conscious efforts — if the gain is to be made essential and intrinsic — becomes ultimately a part of the unconscious mind, and is thus capable of being utilized with instinctive immediacy. Knowledge employed in consecutive logic may be said to be still incompletely acquired and unwedded to one's way of thought: it was somewhat with this implication that John Gregory, for example, stated that "reason" is "a weak principle in Man, in respect of Instinct, and generally is a more unsafe guide"; and that many of man's ills "are entirely the result of our own caprice and folly in paying greater regard to vague and shallow reasonings than to the plain dictates of Instinct."

The ability to digest and render automatic what has been acquired from experience and study is, among the English writers of this group, inherent in the associative process itself; among the Scottish, it is regarded as a general mental capacity, which association abets and complements. And whatever the extent to which it is identified, by various writers, with this process or capacity, it is at least a fast-growing assumption that the imagination draws, without the need of consecutive analysis, upon associational instincts which have been broadened and matured by experience. And since it is founded directly upon an associational union and concert of many aspects or "faculties" of thought, it is able to bring the mind to focus, as it were, from several positions at once: it thus not only possesses a perpetual immediacy in its conception of its particular object, but it is also capable of a superior comprehensiveness as well. The imagination, stated one of the members of the Scottish school, conceives its object

with all its qualities and circumstances . . . in respect to all their relations of similitude, analogy, or opposition; whereas, in abstraction, we would consider subjects, or *parts* of subjects, in some *limited* point of view, to which our reasoning or thought in that instance is directed.[19]

If the "imagination" in its completed state be analyzed, said Dugald Stewart, it will be found to employ several "faculties," including

Conception or simple Apprehension, which enables us to form a notion of those former objects of perception or of knowledge, out of which we are to make a selection; Abstraction, which separates the selected materials; . . . and Judgment or Taste, which selects the materials, and directs their combination. To these powers, we may add that particular habit of association to which I formerly gave the name of Fancy.

Thus, in Milton's portrayal of the Garden of Eden, the associative and aggregative power of "fancy" suggested to him

a variety of the most striking scenes which he had seen . . . and the power of Conception placed each of them before him with all its beauties and imperfections. In every natural scene, if we destine it for any particular purpose, there are defects and redundancies. . . . Milton, accordingly, would not copy his Eden from any one scene, but would select from each. . . . The power of Abstraction enabled him to make the separation, and Taste directed him in the selection.[20]

[19] Adam Ferguson, "Imagination," *Principles of Moral and Political Science* (Edinburgh: 1792), I, 104.
[20] Dugald Stewart, "Of Imagination," *Elements of the Philosophy of the Human Mind* (Edinburgh: 1792), pp. 477–478.

Somewhat indicative of this attitude is the contention of such
Scottish critics as Alexander Gerard and John Ogilvie that, in any
gifted and fruitful aesthetic effort, whether creative or appreciative, judgment and imagination work simultaneously and not in
succession. The contention is hardly peculiar to the associationist
critics, of course: Quintilian had made it, and, among neo-classic
critics, it was more or less assumed by Johnson and certainly by
Reynolds.

VI

English romantic criticism, in addition to finding immediacy
and comprehensiveness in the associative process, proceeded upon
the assumption that the subjectively creative function of association also possesses a valid insight into the *total* nature of its object. For while logical analysis tends to render piecemeal, and,
except for an almost artificial order of its own, to leave something
of a disunity in the trail of its dissection, the associative imagination is essentially *synthetic* in its conception, and, however numerous the component parts of which it takes cognizance, grasps its
object as the single, unified particular that it is, and presents it
with a similar amalgamated totality. This fundamentally romantic insistence on the ability of the imagination to conceive in terms
of an integrated whole is, in part, one of the offshoots of the doctrine of *coalescence* which was developed by some of the eighteenth-century associationists, assumed by Wordsworth, Coleridge,
and especially Hazlitt, and later designated as "mental chemistry"
by John Stuart Mill and others. The doctrine is distinctively British; and, until after the first quarter of the nineteenth century,
there is no real evidence of its appearance in either the psychology or the romantic criticism of the continent.

As distinct from the mere combination of simple into complex
ideas, "coalescence" signifies a fusion of sensations or ideas into
an entirely new and irreducible whole. This doctrine had been
briefly hinted at by John Gay and later extended by Hartley;

but neither stressed very much the element of novelty and uniqueness in a coalesced result. The first detailed if somewhat scattered exposition of this theory was given by Abraham Tucker, from whom it was directly taken over into some of the romantic criticism of a generation later. If a series of logical steps leads to a certain conclusion, those steps may in time "lapse" or become simply absorbed, so to speak, into what follows, with the result that premise and conclusion will ultimately stand forth as a single "intuitive" feeling or thought. The same may be true of almost any kind of conception. Hartley and Priestley, for example, had cited the "coalescence" of language as an illustration: particular letters become fused into syllables, and syllables into words; words, again, become coalesced into phrases which possess distinctive meanings; and an entirely new significance apart from that of the individual letters, syllables, or even words, is thus given these specific elements as they combine and blend together.

This associational tendency largely accounts for the imagination's capacity, which romantic critics were increasingly to stress, not merely to recompose from original elements but, as a kind of "shaping spirit," to present a wholly new creation; for "a compound," stated Tucker, "may have properties resulting from the composition which do not belong to the parts singly whereof it consists." A common analogy employed is the formation of an entirely new color by the mixing of others, and especially the fusion into whiteness of all the colors of the spectrum. Yet these new properties, which some romantic writers assumed could be best conveyed in art by the use of "suggestion," are valid: they are such as accrue from the very nature of the unity of the separate parts, and are consequently what characterize a specific object as the individual particular which it is. Tucker's assumption thus bears at least a superficial resemblance to those upon which the recent theories of "holism" and of the *Gestalt* psychology rest. For "holism" maintains that, just as in chemical compounds, the properties of any unit qualitatively transcend the mere aggregate or sum of the properties of its various parts; and, with a similar point of view, the *Gestalt* or "configurationist" psychology emphasizes the new and irreducible unity of any "pattern" of phenomena.

Although Tucker's theory implies the existence of a distinctive total nature of any particular, the fusion of which he speaks is a mental and even subjective process. This process begins with the coalescing of simple sensations. For example, "the taste of sugar in our mouths joins with the colour we saw before putting it in and the hardness we felt while he held it in our hands"; and together these ideas form the unified "complex of sugar." Further qualities may in time be "melted" into this single conception, such as "that sugar is brittle, dissolvable, clammy, and astringent." This imaginative coalescence of simple sensations, when once achieved, stands in perpetual readiness, as it were, to supplement and render more accurate and significant any single perception of the particular. Thus Tucker, employing one of Berkeley's familiar illustrations, pointed out that, although "we talk of seeing cubes and globes, . . . in reality our sense exhibits no such objects to the mind": in viewing a cube, we can at most see only three sides, and we can perceive only one hemisphere of a globe. It is the associative working of the "imagination," drawing upon the stores of past experience and coalescing these remembrances with the simple sensation of the object, which

supplies what is wanting to compleat their figures. It has been said that all things strike the eye in a flat surface, and that our former acquaintance with the objects makes them appear standing out one before another: thus much is certain that the figures lie level in a picture, wherefore the roundness and protuberance we discern in them cannot come from the sense but must be drawn from our internal fund.[21]

In proportion to both experience and imaginative strength, this coalescence will enlarge in comprehensiveness, and still be capable

[21] *Light of Nature*, I, 230.

of instinctive and immediate control in one's conception or judgment of any phenomena, aesthetic or otherwise:

As our acquaintance with objects increases, we add fresh ingredients to the compounds formed of them in our imagination; therefore those we have occasion the most frequently to consider become the most comprehensive assemblages. By this means, manufacturers, artisans, scholars, and others following any particular occupation have a fuller idea of the *things* belonging to their respective trades or sciences.[22]

Thus, to most people, the "whole complex of gold" consists of its "yellowness, hardness, and valuableness in commerce," whereas in the "complex" idea of the goldsmith or the refiner, such qualities as maleability, ductility, and the like are added. Again, a conception of the *Iliad* may begin as "no more than the story of an old siege wrote in Greek verse; but together with this there arises in the mind of the poet or critic ideas of the fable, the characters, the sentiment, the diction . . ."

By thus controlling perception, associative coalescence may perhaps be said to subjectify it; but this subjectively controlled perception is still more valid in its insight than is the working of piecemeal logic. For just as the most primary qualities are grasped in their unity, so other characteristics gradually learned through experience are seen by an active imagination not only as intrinsic elements of a whole but as being actually *in* the object of which they are indeed a part — each element, quality, or ramification imparting its distinctive "flavor" or "tincture" to that entirely new coalescence which is the reality, the true nature, of the object contemplated. By thus centering its knowledge in the particular, "to which alone are the strongest sensations annexed," the coalescing power of association also insures a persuasive vigor of realization. With sufficient imaginative strength and knowledge of human nature, for example, one could "scarce look a stranger in the face," wrote Tucker, "without entertaining some

[22] *Ibid.*, I, 233–234.

notion of his character and temper of mind" — an ability which
Hazlitt was later to find so well exemplified by Shakespeare. And
indeed if this capacity — which underlies the immediate working
of taste as well as of all other judgment — is sufficiently developed, the individual "expression" in any object may be at once
discerned in its total potentiality, and be unerringly employed as
the key to the distinctive and specific character of that particular.

VII

The doctrine of "coalescence," especially as it was evolved by
Tucker, can hardly be said to have influenced English criticism
strongly until almost the close of the eighteenth century. It is
to be viewed as a manifestation, rather, of the larger assumption
which increasingly affected the English romantic conception of
taste or aesthetic evaluation — the more general assumption that
an immediate, comprehensive, and unified conception of the particular is achieved through an instinctive employment of experience. But this conceptual power of unifying association can do
more than discern and present the particular in a total synthesis,
and with the various aspects of its nature impressed, as it were,
upon it. The associative capacity, interrelating as it does all functions and faculties of thought, is also aware of whatever added
character its object assumes from any relationships or analogies
it may have with other specific phenomena: it comprehends, in
other words, that pertinent arrangement, interconnection, or mutual influence of various particulars which, in the aesthetic realm,
comprises fitness, design, pattern, or, in the larger sense, form.

This conception of the potential relationship of particulars in
a larger whole or towards a given end is achieved by a dominant
association which acts as a controlling and unifying purpose. The
proportion to which the form or interrelation thus conceived is
valid and pertinent depends in part upon the extent to which this
dominant association is fundamental and free from accidental circumstance. Thus the interplay of mutual influence which is per-

ceived by the association of *cause and effect* is more generally significant than is a relationship by *resemblance;* and the perceptions of *resemblance* and *contrariety* are less liable, in turn, to be irrelevant to the object and to be colored by extraneous and artificial conditions than are the associations which are determined merely by *contiguity* or *vicinity,* and which tend to be the predominant ones in people of weak imagination. A favorite illustration of the slightness and scattered irrelevance of association by mere vicinity is Dame Quickly's reply to Falstaff's question, "What is the gross sum that I owe thee?" — an illustration first employed by Lord Kames and later by other Scottish critics. Dame Quickly's answer, of course, is "thyself and thy money too." The events by which she recalls the occasion when he promised marriage, "have no other connection with the subject of discourse," as Alexander Gerard said, "but this, that they happened in the place and at the time to which it refers":

Thou didst swear to me upon a parcel-gilt goblet, sitting in my Dolphinchamber, at the round table, by a sea-coal fire, upon Wednesday in Wheeson week, when the prince broke thy head for liking his father to a singing-man of Windsor, thou didst swear to me then, as I was washing thy wound, to marry me, and make me my lady thy wife. Canst thou deny it? Did not goodwife Keech, the butcher's wife, come in then . . . to borrow a mess of vinegar; telling us she had a good dish of prawns; whereby thou didst desire to eat some, whereby I told thee they were ill for a green wound? And didst thou not, when she was gone downstairs, desire me to be no more so familiar with such poor people; saying that ere long they should call me "madam"? And didst thou not kiss me and bid me fetch thee thirty shillings? [23]

The premise of associationism, moreover, that the significance of interrelationship itself, like all other phenomena, is grasped by an instinctive capacity which has been matured through habit and wide experience, was far from incompatible with the growing romantic insistence that emotion necessarily accompanies and

[23] *Henry IV*, Pt. II, II, 1.

abets the working of that insight. Indeed, an occasional anticipation may be found of the romantic assumption that the riveting of associational conception to its object, with a resulting union of both object and its external relationships into the organic totality which they naturally comprise, is largely initiated and accelerated by the influence of the "passions." Such an anticipation may be especially typified by Alexander Gerard's *Essay on Genius* (1774), which elaborated and analyzed suggestions he had made in his earlier *Essay on Taste* (1759).

Every passion, said Gerard, tends to suggest and even force into view whatever ideas are related to it, such as "the object of the passion, its cause, what is fit for supporting it, or what gratifies it": thus, in a state of extreme anger, a man "can scarce avoid thinking of the person who has offended him, and of the injury he has done him, recollecting everything he can dishonourable to that person, . . . and in a word dwelling on everything immediately relating to his anger." All ideas, in short, which are congruous to a specific state of feeling, exist, as it were, "in a continual readiness." Still, a passion gives a unity to these related ideas by bringing them back to itself: it keeps "the attention fixt on the objects strictly connected with it," and it does this "so powerfully and so constantly that the imagination is drawn backwards to repeated conceptions of them."

One of many examples of this, and of Shakespeare's customary understanding of it, may be cited from the *Tempest:* Alonso, the King of Naples, suffers shipwreck on his return from his daughter's marriage with the King of Tunis; he believes his son, who has accompanied him on the trip, to have been lost in the storm; and when Alonso's companions seek to divert his thoughts to the more cheerful subject of his daughter's marriage, he replies:

> You cram these words into mine ears, against
> The stomach of my sense. Would I had never
> Married my daughter there! for, coming thence,
> My son is lost; and, in my rate, she too,

> Who is so far from Italy remov'd,
> I ne'er again shall see her. O thou, mine heir
> Of Naples and of Milan! . . .[24]

The passion of grief keeps Alonso's attention directed to the loss of his son — the object which is associated with the passion as being its immediate cause. But the loss of his son, said Gerard, in turn suggests *its* cause, the marriage at Tunis; for had there been no marriage, there would have been no journey and no shipwreck. From the marriage, Alonso's thoughts again revert to his son's supposed death

> which, when thus again presented to his imagination, suggests a second time his daughter's marriage, by means of its resemblance to it in one particular, that her distance deprived him of all intercourse with her, as much as if she too had been dead. But sorrow for his son allows him not to rest long upon this thought, suitable as it is to his passion . . .; it makes his imagination instantly to recur to the loss . . . to view it in every light, to conceive many circumstances relating to him, his being his heir, his being entitled to large dominions. . . .[25]

A passion, in short, "preserves us from attending to foreign ideas, which would confound our thoughts and retard our progress"; and when an object is brought into the mind by a passion to which it is related,

> it receives a tincture from that passion, it exerts its power of association only in such ways and so far as the passion permits, . . . it introduces no long train of ideas, but suffers the mind to return quickly to the conception of itself, or of some other object as intimately related to the passion.[26]

It is to be emphasized, of course, that the ideas which a passion or a dominant association forces into view will hardly be the most fruitful nor can their pertinence be called valid or sound un-

[24] *Tempest*, II, 2.
[25] Alexander Gerard, "Of the Influence of the Passions on Association," *An Essay on Genius* (1774), pp. 163–164.
[26] *Ibid.*, p. 170.

less the associative capacity has been schooled and broadened by knowledge. The contention is simply that, if such an enlargement has been made and if sufficient knowledge has been acquired and rendered habitual, then a passion or strongly dominant association consolidates all the subordinate relationships with itself, and bestows upon them an organic unity and vital immediacy. It is in this sense that an associational purpose guides the intuitional grasp of that "proper adaptation of means to an end" which comprises form, design, and "fitness." What some of the Shaftesburyans as well as the associationists called the *magnet-like* capacity of the imagination — its ability to draw to itself, with unconscious felicity, all that is strictly relevant to its intention — arises from the almost emotional desire for satisfaction which attends upon a firmly-held idea of any purpose, end, or form. As Tucker pointed out, in one of the homely illustrations which so gratified Hazlitt,

An idea on being displaced by another does not wholly vanish, but leaves a spice or tincture of itself behind, by which it operates with a kind of attraction upon the subsequent ideas, determining which of their associates they shall introduce, namely, such as carry some conformity with itself. Thus if on going to market to buy oats for your horse, you meet a waggon on the way, it might suggest the idea of other carriages, of turnpike roads, of commerce . . . [But] your horse's wants, being already in your thoughts, confine them to take a course relative thereto: so the waggon puts you in mind of the owner being a considerable farmer who may supply you more conveniently and cheaply than the market . . .[27]

For although subordinate relations, when known and felt by the associative faculty, exert their own distinctive "forces," yet "the predominate one," as Gerard maintained, "gives their exertions a particular direction . . . it, as it were, infuses its own spirit into them"; for every associational principle is capable of being modified, and the "predominant principle" so prepares one's

[27] Tucker, *Light of Nature*, I, 246.

disposition of mind that only those modifications of the subordinate principles which are severely pertinent to the desired end, and which are "fittest for promoting its designs," will be felt.

When knowledge and experience have been sufficiently inculcated, therefore, this associational control by a central passion, object, or purpose, with its admission of those ideas alone which have strict and natural relevance to it, results in "regularity," "justness," or "fitness" of form; and should any idea be suggested which is not conducive to the central design, the emotionally predominant

conception of this design breaks in of its own accord, and, like an antagonist muscle, counteracting the other association, draws us off to the view of a more proper idea.

In this manner an attachment to the design naturally produces . . . regularity of imagination, [the] capacity of avoiding foreign, useless, and superfluous conceptions, at the same time that none necessary or proper are passed by. . . .[28]

Almost as "acuteness of smell carries a dog along the path of the game . . . so this happy structure of imagination," said Gerard, proceeds with an "instinctive infallibility" which prevents the mind "from turning aside to wander in improper roads." "Judgment" — though whatever aid it has to render is already being used when the entire associational function is brought into play — can, when acting separately, at best only passively note "the rectitude and errors" of construction and design, and merely reflect upon those natural relations with which the imagination has already been "affected." And as its naturalness and authenticity depend on the extensiveness and vigor of instinctive associational response, the successful interweaving of external relationships and analogies into an ordered design or purpose is therefore far from being coolly circumspect, reflective, and deliberate; together with the added truth and breadth of insight and representation which are its accompaniment, it is itself an organic part

[28] Gerard, "How Genius Arises from the Imagination," *Essay on Genius*, p. 47.

of imaginative creation and indeed of aesthetic understanding in general.

Although it strongly abetted the generally increasing empirical reliance on individual experience and on the particular, associationism illustrated the existence, therefore, of an instinctive capacity to absorb, combine, and guide the ideas which the experience of the particular achieves. It consequently sanctioned and even satisfied the hope for a spontaneous immediacy in imaginative conception, and at the same time it attempted to prove the possibility of a more or less comprehensive understanding of the particular, both in its individual "coalesced" entirety, and in the significance which it assumes for the human mind by its relationships with other objects. Aesthetic criticism, robbed though it was of its confidence in the rational grasp of the ideal, was thus given at least an empirically explainable basis for the creation and understanding of art. But by encouraging aesthetics to take the subjective activity of the mind as the starting point of any investigation, British associationism opened the door even more widely for an inevitable individualistic relativism. In doing so, it substantiated a tendency which was to be even more characteristic of the romantic thought of the following century: a tendency to emphasize the fundamental importance of individual feeling or sentiment.

CHAPTER V.

THE GROWTH OF INDIVIDUALISM: THE PREMISE OF FEELING

←————————————————————————————————————→

"Poetry," said Wordsworth, "is the history, or science, of the feelings"; for it is the "heart" which seeks "the light of truth." A rather general reliance on feeling as a valid means of insight and communication accompanied the earlier stages of the increased relativism which, in varying guises and degrees, has tended to dominate western art since the latter part of the eighteenth century. It is an ironic commonplace of intellectual history that one of the major sources of the romantic stress on feeling was ultimately the mechanistic psychology of the seventeenth and eighteenth centuries. Empiricism, having disposed of the mind as a strictly rational instrument, was increasingly forced to fall back on the immediate feeling of the individual. "What is commonly, and in a popular sense, called reason," said Hume, "is nothing but a general and a calm passion which takes a comprehensive and distant view of its object"; and "what we call *strength of mind*," for example, is only "the prevalence of the calm passions above the violent." Despite the admittedly extreme position of Hume, it is significant that even those who opposed him, such as the members of the Scottish "Common-Sense" School, urged an intuitionalism which had a strongly emotional tinge. In general, the copious British writing of the eighteenth century on sentiment or feeling, and on the use which intuition makes of it, simply anticipated Kant — who of course drew heavily on it in his earlier work — in its desire to find or reconstruct some general basis for knowledge, morality, and art.

As it reflected and abided by this general empirical tendency,

English aesthetic criticism increasingly verged towards the subjective emotionalism which had been advocated or implied by the *je ne sais quoi* "School of Taste" and by Shaftesbury and his ardent following. Stemming from Shaftesbury, a modified confidence in an "inner sense" passed almost imperceptibly, especially through the Scottish school of moralists and critics, into much of later eighteenth-century British thought. But what had before been rather confusedly and impulsively advanced by critics of the *je ne sais quoi* faith and by the early Shaftesburyans now received psychological support. Associationism, in particular, tended to give such a support by breaking down the barrier between "thought" and "feeling": by considering thought and conviction as an intricately interrelated series of feelings and responses on the part of the human mechanism to an external stimulus. A parallel tendency had already begun in France, with the importation of Locke's sensationalism. "How many excellent philosophers," said La Mettrie, in his *Man as a Machine,* "have now shown that thought is but a faculty of feeling!" Whether the position was taken that the emotional response to the good and the beautiful is the function of an innate sense, which is unerring in its insight; or whether, in another extreme, this response was viewed as simply the accumulated result of habit and experience, and as merely the sole means of cognition possible under the circumstances, a general standpoint gradually assumed is that which Goethe permitted Faust to utter in the often-abused statement, "Feeling is all."

Feeling transcends what is usually regarded as "reason," not only because it offers a more spontaneous vitality of realization, but also because it is aware of nuances of significance and of interrelationship to which the logical process is impervious. Certain realities, stated a Scottish writer, John Gregory, necessarily defy strictly mental cognition; there is, for example, "a correspondence between certain external forms of Nature, and certain affections of the Mind, that may be *felt,* but cannot be explained."

Abraham Tucker, again, maintained that we can only "reason *about*" such a phenomenon as "force"; and the implication of his entire conception of the imagination is that, because of its fluidity and elusiveness compared with the fixed character of human "reason," such an aspect of nature as "force" cannot be known and divulged except by a feeling through direct experience. The primary characteristic of empirical reality is flux and change; the reasoning process *abstracts* and *categorizes* conclusions from this flux, and bestows on them an artificial rigidity and a static order of its own. It is in this sense that Wordsworth referred to the intellect as "meddling," and that Keats stated "I am certain of nothing but the holiness of the Heart's affections and the truth of the Imagination. . . . I have never yet been able to perceive how anything can be known for truth by consequitive reasoning." By "feeling," said the noted German prophet of romanticism, August Wilhelm von Schlegel, one becomes aware of the subtlest and most fluid interrelationships between objects or between ideas: "The ancient art and poetry rigorously separate things which are dissimilar; the romantic delights in indissoluble mixtures." Classicism conceives the world as exhibiting the harmonious legislation of law and order, and as

reflecting in itself the eternal images of things. Romantic poetry, on the other hand, is the expression of a secret attraction to a chaos which lies concealed . . . and is perpetually striving after new and marvellous births. . . . The former is more simple, clear, and like to nature in the self-existent perfection of its works; the latter . . . approaches more to the secret of the universe. For Conception can only comprise each object separately, but nothing in truth can ever exist separately and by itself; *Feeling* perceives all in all at one and the same time.[1]

II

The evolution of the romantic stress on feeling as a means of effective insight may be characteristically illustrated by the increas-

[1] August Wilhelm von Schlegel, *Lectures on Dramatic Art and Literature* (1809–1811), Lect. xxii.

ing rôle assigned to sympathy in both moral and aesthetic theory. It is one of the common tenets of English romantic criticism that the imagination is capable, through an effort of sympathetic intuition, of identifying itself with its object; and, by means of this identification, the sympathetic imagination grasps, through a kind of direct experience and feeling, the distinctive nature, identity, or "truth" of the object of its contemplation. The critical opinions of Wordsworth, Coleridge, and several minor critics frequently reveal this assumption. Hazlitt, as Mr. Bullitt has shown, made it the basis not only of his conception of the imagination but of his ethics, and there is reason to believe that Keats did likewise.

As it finally matured in English romantic thought, and in so far as it was applied to purely aesthetic ends, this conception of sympathy bears certain similarities to the more restricted and specific doctrine of *Einfühlung*, which was developed in Germany at the close of the last century and to which the term "empathy" has since been devoted in English. In British romantic thought generally, however, sympathy had a broad moral application, and played an important part in the attempt to re-establish a bond of union not only among mankind but also between man and external nature. As such, its ramifications were numerous and varied, and extended from its influence on the sober ethics of some of the early-nineteenth-century Scottish school to its predominance in the brilliant interpretation, by Hazlitt and occasionally Keats, of Shakespeare and of the poetic function generally; from its presence in Wordsworth's calm and meditative regard for nature to its subjectively nostalgic and almost nihilistic expression in Byron's occasional identification of himself with the ocean, the storm, and the mountains, or in Shelley's yearning to merge himself in the West Wind. Like other aspects of the romantic emphasis on feeling as a primary means of aesthetic and moral insight and communication, the conception of sympathy as a guiding principle took rise, on the one hand, from the innate sensibility hypothesized by Shaftesbury and his more moderate Scottish followers, and, on the other hand, from empirical associationism.

A belief in the importance of the artist's capacity to enter totally into his subject, with a resulting obliteration of his own identity, is occasionally found in early English neo-classicism. One writer, for example, in the latter half of the seventeenth century, had dwelt upon Shakespeare's ability to "metamorphose" himself into his characters. Shaftesbury, somewhat later, almost anticipated the language of Keats's famous contention that the true poet "has no character . . . no identity," but that he becomes "annihilated" in the characters of those about him and concerns himself with revealing their essential natures. For Shaftesbury, too, considered that in the conception and portrayal of his subject the poet is, ideally speaking, "annihilated," and is "no certain man, nor has any certain or genuine character." In addition to this sort of anticipation of what was later to become a pervasive assumption in much general aesthetic theory, there is also a pronounced tendency, among a few of the earlier intuitional moralists of the eighteenth century, to regard sympathy as an important aid to the "moral sense." For example, James Arbuckle, an admiring disciple of Shaftesbury, considered moral action impossible without the capacity to enter sympathetically into others: man is ultimately controlled by feeling rather than reason; and we may consequently "see the Wisdom of our Creator in giving us this imagining *Faculty,* and such a Facility of placing ourselves in Circumstances different from those we are really in, to enforce our Duty upon us, not only by Reason, but by Passion and powerful Inclination." [2]

The emerging of this moral conception, among some of the benevolists, received a sudden and marked impetus from empiricism; and Hume, who demolished reason as an ethical guide and

[2] James Arbuckle, *Collection of Letters and Essays* (1722), I, 33–34 (No. 4).

yet discovered no distinct "moral sense," resolved almost all moral response into sympathy. It is significant that even Johnson admitted that "all joy or sorrow for the happiness or calamities of others is produced by an act of the imagination, that realizes the event . . . by placing us, for a time, in the condition of him whose fortune we contemplate; so that we feel . . . whatever emotions would be excited by the same good or evil happening to ourselves." Yet sympathy, like any other emotional capacity, was regarded by Johnson as at best a means of enforcing the rational grasp of the universal. Adam Smith particularized and extended the doctrine of sympathy which Hume had advanced; and the design of his *Theory of Moral Sentiments* (1759) is the complete substitution of sympathy for the "moral sense" as man's internal monitor, and the elaboration of it as an all-embracing principle. Moral judgment, for Smith, involved a sympathetic participation with those who would be affected by the external consequences, good or bad, of an act; but it equally necessitated an awareness, through sympathy with the executor of the act, both of the "intention or affection of the heart" from which he acts, and of the specific situation, bodily or mental, which helps to prompt that intention. Although he emphasized the instinctiveness of such sympathetic understanding, and even regarded it as divinely implanted, Smith also recognized the contributing influence of habit and custom. He consequently admitted that a large relativity in sympathetic reaction is bound to result — a relativity determined by the associations which experience teaches and by the inherent sensitivity and capacity of the individual nature. Smith, finally, did not identify his internal monitor with the imagination, but he stressed at the outset the complete inability of the sympathy to function without the imagination:

As we have no immediate experience of what other men feel, we can form no idea of the manner in which they are affected, but by conceiving what we ourselves should feel in the like situation. Though our brother is on the rack, as long as we ourselves are at our ease, our senses will never inform us of what he suffers. They never did and never can carry us beyond our persons, and it is by the imagination that we can form any conception of what are his sensations.[3]

The influence of the *Theory of Moral Sentiments* on British moral thought was suggestive rather than directing. Many contemporary Scottish moralists emphasized the rôle of sympathy as a greatly contributing though by no means sole principle of morality, and, like Dugald Stewart, agreed that the imagination is of fundamental importance to any exercise of sympathy. Among Scottish literary critics, moreover, the book enjoyed a far more widespread vogue. The *Theory of Moral Sentiments* is in some respects hardly more than an indication of a growing moral and aesthetic tendency. Yet the book elaborated and even crystallized some of the assumptions of this tendency, particularly the interworking of sympathy with the imagination; and it is of some significance that the development of the sympathetic imagination as an aesthetic doctrine came largely from a group of Scottish critics who almost agreed with Archibald Alison's estimate of the *Moral Sentiments* as "the most eloquent work on the subject of Morals that Modern Europe has produced," and who felt with James Beattie that "the philosophy of Sympathy ought also to form a part of the science of Criticism."

Among critics who ultimately stem from the "moral sense" school, there is a strong inclination to maintain the intimate connection between imagination and "sensibility," and to assume, as John Ogilvie did, that "in proportion to the degree in which one takes place, will be always the poignancy and edge of the other." Extreme sensibility, and a consequent "enthusiasm" on the part of the poet, whether they were psychologically a part of imaginative action itself or whether they were externally complementary in their working with it, were especially necessary for the complete self-absorption of the poet in the object of his con-

[3] Adam Smith, *Theory of Moral Sentiments* (2nd ed., 1762), p. 2.

cern, and for the sympathetic understanding which he achieves by means of this absorption.

The general eighteenth-century principle that, in order to comprehend and represent nature, one must possess above all an extensive knowledge of human nature in its various ramifications is naturally assumed as a necessary qualification for genuine sympathy. As Beattie, echoing Adam Smith, pointed out, we sympathize with what we know; and the wider our knowledge and experience, the wider is the scope of our sympathy and the juster and more accurate it is in perceiving the character and significance of its object. Yet the broadest knowledge of mankind, Beattie added, would not have enabled a poet like Blackmore to portray such characters as Homer's Achilles, Shakespeare's Othello, or Milton's Satan; for the hapless Blackmore was not endowed with that "sensibility" which "must first of all engage him warmly in his subject." The poet who aspires for lasting reputation "must not only study nature, and know the reality of things; but he must possess . . . sensibility, to enter with ardent enthusiasm into every part of his subject, so as to transfuse into his work a pathos and energy sufficient to raise corresponding emotions in his reader." Indeed, it is sensibility and "enthusiastic delight" which make fruitful and even possible the knowledge won from experience; enthusiasm rivets the attention; "He best shall paint them" — he quotes from Pope — "who can feel them most"; for close and accurate observation of nature, sustained over any period of time, "is to be expected from those only who take pleasure in it." And in one of his later works Beattie even maintained that sympathy was not only indispensable to poetic creation, but that, together with "liveliness" and "distinct apprehension" of imagination, it comprises "taste" itself; and if a reader lack "sympathy, it will be impossible for him to receive any true pleasure from a good poem, however skilled he may be in language and versification, and however well acquainted with the ordinary appearances of nature."

In successful sympathetic identification, whether directed to a moral or an aesthetic end, the necessary qualifications, on the one hand, of instinctive sensibility and imaginative fervor, and, on the other, of extensive acquaintance with human nature, are not to be viewed as separate in their use; they together comprise a single intuition, immediate and inevitable in its procedure, but none the less sagacious and informed. The distinctively British yoking of empiricism and intuitionalism, so frequently present in the whole of British philosophy, was especially assumed by critics who emphasized the importance of sympathetic participation. "Exquisite sensibility" and "the most copious imagination," said John Ogilvie, must be extensively schooled and disciplined by study and practical experience. This union of feeling, imagination, and experience constitutes "discernment," by means of which the poet is capable of

entering deeply into the characters of those with whom he is conversant. He gains a facility of reading in the countenance those sensations, however closely concealed, that actuate the heart; and of collecting from casual, loose, and unsupported assertions thrown out apparently at random . . . such significant and distinguishing criteria as are decisive of their justness, propriety, and importance.[4]

However variously it may have shown itself in their works, said Ogilvie, "this facility of entering deeply into the feelings of the heart distinguishes principally those authors who will always stand in the highest rank of eminence"; and he would have agreed with Beattie that the verdict of time illustrates that no work of art "can give lasting delight to a moral being, but that which awakens sympathy." This faculty of identification is necessary not only in the creation of art, but also for taste itself. The general disposition of a critic of genuine taste is

[4] John Ogilvie, *Philosophical and Critical Observations on the Nature, Characters, and Various Species of Composition* (1774), I, 178, 282–283, and *passim*.

characterized by no circumstance more remarkably than its power of entering into a character when supplied with slight materials, and such as an ordinary mind would wholly overlook. . . . Thus it is that a discerning critic, attentive to the first dawning of genius, will discover in a few loose thoughts thrown out without much connection, the characters of an accurate or comprehensive understanding; and from a few strokes in the same manner of pathos or of description, will judge of the future extent, fertility, and even of the characteristical bias of imagination.[5]

But "discernment," whatever the elements that constitute it, is a single and integrated intuition: in seizing upon the interior workings of the mind and feelings of the person with whom it has become identified, it follows them "through all their windings, and the effects arising from each, however complicated," with an automatic immediacy; and it achieves a coalesced unity which cannot be grasped rationally or "by considering separately each particular part, however necessary to constitute a whole."

The instinctive working of sympathy and its prevalence in one form or another were further substantiated by British associationism. "Since the mind," said Joseph Priestley, "perceives, and is conscious of nothing, but the ideas that are present to it, it must, as it were, *conform* itself to them": dependent as it is upon sensation alone, it adapts itself to the character of what is immediately before it, and does it

so instantaneously and mechanically, that no person whatever hath reflection . . . to be upon his guard against some of the most useless and ridiculous effects of it. What person, if he saw another upon a precipice and in danger of falling, could help starting back, and throwing himself into the same posture as he would do if he himself were going to fall? At least he would have a strong propensity to do it. And what is more common than to see persons in playing at bowls, lean their own bodies, and writhe them into every possible attitude, according to the course

[5] *Ibid.*, I, 220–221.

they would have their bowl to take? . . . The more vivid are a man's
ideas, and the greater is his general sensibility, the more intirely, and
with the greater facility, doth he adapt himself to the situations he is
viewing.[6]

For not only are ideas associated with each other; but, as
many British associationists showed, ideas, sensations, sentiments,
and even muscular motions may all be as easily interrelated with
each other by association; and indeed, the difference between an
idea and a feeling is little more than a difference in intensity of
realization. Thus one critic cited the manner in which Achilles'
anger arises, at the thought of his injury, as revealing Homer's
understanding of "a close linked connexion of ideas and sensations." Just as a certain idea, added Erasmus Darwin, may by
association evoke the passion of anger, and this in turn the appropriate muscular response; so, by a kind of reverse process, if we
assume

the attitude that any passion naturally occasions, we soon in some degree
acquire that passion; hence when those that scold indulge themselves
in loud oaths, and violent action of the arms, they increase their anger
by the mode of expressing themselves; and on the contrary the counter-
feited smile of pleasure in disagreeable company soon brings along with
it a portion of the reality.

This method of "entering into the passions of others is rendered
of very extensive use by the pleasure we take in imitation." Though
it may vary in degree, intelligence, and scope, a propensity to imitation of some sort is universally instinctive to the human mind;
and it is simply from the same capacity, said Darwin, which underlies

our aptitude for imitation, [that there] arises what is generally understood by the word of sympathy, so well explained by Dr. Smith of Glas-
gow. Thus the appearance of a cheerful countenance gives us pleasure,

---

[6] Joseph Priestley, *Course of Lectures on Oratory and Criticism* (1777), pp.
126–127.

and of a melancholy one makes us sorrowful. Yawning and sometimes vomiting are thus propagated by sympathy, and some people of delicate fibres, at the presence of a spectacle of misery, have felt pain in the same parts of their own bodies, that were diseased or mangled in the other. Amongst the writers of antiquity, Aristotle thought this aptitude to imitation an essential property of the human species, and calls man an imitative animal.[7]

The insistence, by the more mechanistic associationists, that sympathy is an instinctive human response also manifests a growing critical attempt to find a more spontaneous and a more comprehensive means of grasping the distinctive character of a particular, whether it be an object or a person, and then of portraying it through some sort of "expression." In his *Essay on Taste* (1759), Alexander Gerard spoke of an innate "sensibility of heart," by means of which, in poetry and drama, we identify ourselves with the characters "and sympathize with every change in their condition." Hume had always maintained that sympathy "is nothing but the conversion of an idea into an impression by the force of the imagination": if the imagination and the capacity for sensibility are strong enough, in other words, an idea becomes more intensely and therefore more emotionally realized; and this impression, when felt with sufficient vivacity, is in turn fused and transformed into the state of feeling or the general condition which was originally observed. In much the same way, Alexander Gerard implied that sympathy is a kind of general propensity of imagination and feeling which prepares the observer "for readily catching, as by infection, any passion": this propensity or "force of sympathy enlivens our *ideas* of the passions infused by it to such a pitch, as in a manner *converts* them to the passions themselves." These passions, raised in the beholder by the sympathetic observation of the passions of others, in turn catch and dominate his imagination, the performance of which is then comparable to that of a magnetic field:

[7] Erasmus Darwin, "Of Instinct," *Zoonomia* (1794–1796), I, 146–147.

As the magnet selects from a quantity of matter the ferruginous par-
ticles, which happen to be scattered through it, without making an impression on other substances; so imagination, by a similar sympathy,
equally inexplicable, draws out from the whole compass of nature such
ideas as we have occasion for, without attending to any others.[8]

The previous chapter cited the manner in which, according to
Gerard, a "passion" or a dominant association draws to itself,
by an instinctive infallibility, all that is congruous or pertinent to
its object, cause, or general character, and modifies these subordinate associations and directs them to a new and coalesced unity.
The function of sympathy is that it serves as the basis, the medium, through which the passions or dominant associations operate in this almost magnetic creation or response; and according
as sympathy has been broadened and rectified by experience and
knowledge, those passions admitted, and the manner of their
working, will be intellectually, morally, or aesthetically just and
fruitful. This standpoint was later assumed even more by Richard Payne Knight, who took it for granted that practically all
aesthetic pleasure arises from some aspect of "internal sympathy,"
and who especially maintained that it is "only by sympathy" that
the emotions can in any way be connected with "taste."

IV

Sympathy, as an aesthetic conception, hardly tended to sanction an indiscriminate naturalism in art. The strongest sympathies,
said Knight, are evoked by what we most admire. Thus, "it is
not with the agonies of a man writhing in the pangs of death,
that we sympathize, on beholding the celebrated group of Laocoön
and his sons; . . . but it is with the energy and fortitude of
mind, which those agonies call into action and display." [9] Similarly,
the characters portrayed, he later stated, must be such that either

[8] Alexander Gerard, *Essay on Taste* (1759), pp. 173–174.
[9] Richard Payne Knight, "Of the Passions," *An Analytical Inquiry into the
Principles of Taste* (2nd ed., 1805), p. 335.

liking or esteem is in some way present; it is solely with certain "energies of mind" of which we approve, and which are revealed by the character under generally significant circumstances, that any lasting sympathy can be had; and if such characters are completely absent, a dramatic work of art fails to call forth any genuine or widespread interest and, despite whatever merit it may otherwise have, becomes a temporary amusement.

At the same time, however, the doctrine of sympathy lent a strong encouragement to a certain verisimilitude of particular representation. For we also, said Beattie, sympathize with what we know: we realize what we see in the concrete more vividly than what we hear described; and accordingly a marked contrast was often drawn by some of the critics of the period between "representation" and "description." "Our sympathy," said Lord Kames, "is not raised by description. . . . It is this imperfection, . . . in the bulk of our plays, that confines our stage almost entirely to Shakespeare." "Naturalness" can be achieved, added Hugh Blair, only if the artist possesses "the power of entering deeply into the character he draws, of becoming for a moment the very person whom he exhibits, and of assuming all his feelings"; and he cited various dramas of the period as examples of the complete lack of this quality, and of the consequent use of the dialogue as a means of "describing" the characters rather than "representing" them. Homer was occasionally cited as the outstanding example of a sympathetic discernment strong enough to represent "natural" characters; but there was more disposition to agree with James Beattie, who considered that Shakespeare possessed so powerful a capacity to enter into his characters that, had he not employed comic admixture, his tragedies would have been too intense for any "person of sensibility" to watch. Shakespeare, said Elizabeth Montagu, had "the art of the Dervise, in the Arabian tales, who could throw his soul into the body of another man, and be at once possessed of his sentiments, adopt his passions, and rise to all the functions and feelings of his situation."

Such statements foreshadow Keats's famous designation of Shakespeare as a man of great "negative capability," and Hazlitt's statement of him that

> He was nothing in himself; but he was all that others were, or that they could become. He not only had in himself the germs of every faculty and feeling, but he could follow them by anticipation, intuitively, into all their conceivable ramifications, through every change of fortune, or conflict of passion, or turn of thought. . . . He had only to think of anything in order to become that thing, with all the circumstances belonging to it.[10]

Sympathy, then, is elicited by the "natural" particular and not by what is generally or abstractly described. Yet in its conception of the particular, sympathetic understanding, since momentary reactions are only partial disclosures of a character, is not confined to the present: sentiments, associations, and motives will always depend on the antecedent state of mind, and the sympathetic imagination will grasp this progressive interworking in the characters which are its subject; in its portrayal of distress, for example, it will suggest, as Gerard said, "such circumstances of former prosperity as aggravate the present distress" — for this very aggravation is a part of the distinctive nature of the distress as it now is. Such imaginative projection, then, will "blend" together the past and present, and, said Ogilvie, perceive and exhibit the natural outlets, however small, which a disposition in the character will take, and "the influence of habit, prepossession, . . . and other such causes as contribute to form a variety of minds particularly investigated." For employing as it does the automatic "coalescing" capacity of association, sympathetic projection may be assumed to detect these aspects, ramifications, and disclosures of character, not as piecemeal or intellectually anatomized phenomena, but as being intrinsically centered in the concrete particular with which it has identified itself.

[10] William Hazlitt, *Lectures on the English Poets* (1818–1819), *Works* (ed. Howe, 1931–1934), V, 47–48.

Romanticism extended the feeling of sympathy to a participation in external nature as well. "If a Sparrow comes before my Window," said Keats, "I take part in its existence and pick about the Gravel"; and he also spoke of the poet as

> the man who with a bird,
> Wren, or Eagle, finds his way to
> All its instincts.

The feeling for animals, however, was less definitely sympathetic than Keats would indicate, and tended to be an outflow of vague fellow-feeling rather than actual identification. We may recall, if a bit unfairly, such unfortunately extreme examples as Coleridge's address to the ass — "I hail thee *Brother*" — or Wordsworth's Peter Bell, who repents through sympathy with an ass, and asks

> When shall I be as good as thou?
> Oh! would, poor beast, that I had now
> A heart but half as good as thine!

It was in this more general and sentimental vein that the feeling for animals was occasionally reflected in the later eighteenth century. An associationist critic, Thomas Percival, felt, for example, that Dyer's unfortunate poem on sheep and the wool trade, *The Fleece* (1757), often neglected opportunities to exploit sympathy to its most exquisite pitch. Percival, who reminds one of such earlier benevolists as John Gilbert Cooper, said he had been "informed that, after the dam has been shorn, and turned into the fold to her lambs, they become estranged to her, and that a scene of reciprocal distress ensues; which a man of lively imagination, and tender feelings, might render highly interesting and pathetic." Lawrence Sterne, he added, would not have neglected such an opportunity; and Percival, who perhaps would have shared Walt Whitman's desire to "turn and live with the animals," became so moved by the prospect that he himself composed and inserted in his criticism the missing scene written "in the manner of Sterne."

Moreover, said Beattie, "We sympathize . . . even with things inanimate. To lose a staff we have long worn, to see in ruins a house in which we have long lived, may affect us . . . though in point of value the loss be nothing." Sympathy with the inanimate arises if we possess a "lively conception" of its significance or end. "Things inanimate," Wordsworth later said, can "speak to social reason's inner sense, With inarticulate language." It is in this respect that he achieved a gayety of spirits in the "jocund company" of the daffodils; and that during his youth, as he wrote in the *Prelude*, he

> was mounting now
> To such community with highest truth —
> A track pursuing, not untrod before,
> From strict analogies by thought supplied
> Or consciousnesses not to be subdued.
> To every natural form, rock, fruit, or flower,
> Even the loose stones that cover the highway,
> I gave a moral life: *I saw them feel*,
> Or *linked them to some feeling*.

A less effusive but more mechanically mimetic identification with the inanimate may extend to such phenomena as force or even form. "Sublimity," for example, has at all times the general association of power, whether magnitude, grandeur, or simply strength of emotion be the means by which it is communicated. Through a kind of identification with objects which have this association of great power, the consequent "expansion of mind" in the beholder results in a feeling of "noble pride." We may recall Richard Wagner's later almost empathic interpretation of the sublime in his essay on Beethoven. The mind, given expanse, finds its own power and that in which it participates combined. For since Lockean sensationalism has taught us that the mind is conscious only of the ideas that are present to it, the mind must, said Priestley, "conform" itself to them:

and even the idea it hath of its own extent . . . must enlarge or contract with its field of view. By this means also, a person, for the time, enters into, adopts, and is actuated by the sentiments that are presented to his mind. . . . From this principle . . . ideas of our *own* greatness, dignity, and importance, are the result of our contemplating large and grand objects. This will be conspicuous when we consider the sublime.[11]

And these feelings of pride, of dignity, of expansion, elicited through identification, are projected upon the object or force and help to give it the character of sublimity. Moreover, aesthetic susceptibility to what we designate as "form" in classical sculpture, said Richard Payne Knight, arises as much from "mental sympathies" as does the pleasure from more individualistic portrayal: however general and ideal the representation, and however lacking may be individual "expression," the observer associates certain postures and general contours with specific "passions and dispositions of mind"; through his associations, his sympathies are elicited and read, so to speak, into the original aesthetic form.

Yet there is also an awareness that an associative identification may be achieved with even simple form as such. Keats, for example, later said that he could almost project himself into a moving billiard-ball, and conceive, as though these qualities were his own, its combined "roundness, smoothness and volubility and the rapidity of its motion." We have, said Lord Kames, an inherent and rather empathic "sense of order and arrangement": "Thinking upon a body in motion, we follow its natural course. The mind falls with a heavy body, descends with a river, and ascends with flame and smoke." Thus, with the serpentine or winding line: slow motion in gentle curves has associations of "Volition

[11] Joseph Priestley, *A Course of Lectures on Oratory and Criticism* (1777), pp. 126–127.

and Ease"; in following the curving of the line with the eye, and hence, Archibald Alison seems to have implied, by a kind of joining in with its motion, we attribute these same associations to the line itself, and we designate it as "beautiful." A similar intimation is that the associations of power which come with the extended sweep of rapid motion are carried over to forms which, for example, possess "magnitude in height": this extensive upward rising lifts the mind; it produces a feeling, said Alison, of "elevation"; and we consequently tend to specify the form that initiates the feeling as "sublime."

The discussion by a few associationists of the reaction of feeling to sound seems to have involved, in a very general way, the same assumption of a kind of sympathetic participation; and as such it foreshadowed an attitude towards music which Schopenhauer and other nineteenth-century German philosophers even further subjectivized. There is a "natural correspondence between movement and passion," said one critic, and "the imagination may be *raised* by movements of expansion." For feeling itself exists in flux, and the acceleration and deepening of its natural ebb and flow by the movement of music or even by a simple sound may perhaps be attributed to the manner in which feeling makes itself specific in the temporal stream, and gives itself form and embodiment through a unification with the flow of sound. It was perhaps with this assumption that Alison could state that the rise and fall through time of a "low, grave sound" is "beautiful"; while in the gradual swelling of a "loud, grave, lengthened, and increasing sound," with its suggestion of power and of "great expansion," the flow of feeling, itself receiving through the participation an embodied expansion and elevation, is such that we characterize the sound as "sublime."

v

Whether it was applied to a virtual associative identification, or to an inner mechanical and mimetic conformity with an object or sound, or whether it revealed itself as merely a vague and frankly subjective outflow of sentiment, the development of the conception of sympathy may be cited as distinctively illustrating the manner in which empirical associationism befriended and combined with emotional intuitionalism. It may also serve, at least in some of its aspects, as a very characteristic example of the attempt to find, in the welter of individual and subjective response, some valid means of both moral and aesthetic understanding — a means, moreover, by which the direct impression of experience could be drawn upon. But if feeling transcends the logical process by sympathetically detecting and realizing qualities in the external world, it can also discern and satisfy more subjective values and reactions which are no less real. Analogies, for example, need not conform to strictly rational demands: what might logically appear as the most diverse phenomena may excite the same feeling and consequently form analogies which, though they obviously exist to the human organism alone, are none the less true and valid simply because they *are* human responses. The employment of these analogies in art is thus not only justifiable; it may even be said to reveal a certain truth about the nature of subjective feeling itself and also to show a fuller significance, in human terms, in any phenomenon which is portrayed.

One of the most characteristic indications of this romantic attitude was a growing concern with what has since been called "synaesthesia": perceptions which come by means of different senses may strike a common emotional note; it is the subjective emotion which is important rather than the perception; and greater subtlety and richer scope may be attained in any art by exploiting this communality of impression and overcoming the division of the senses. The interworking of the senses, as an aesthetic goal, attained considerable vogue on the continent during the nineteenth century: Wagner's *Gesammtkunst*, or "art-work of the future," in which the separate arts are to be fused together, is characteristic of it; and Irving Babbitt has illustrated its extensive appearance in France and the occasionally amusing extremes it reached there.

Synaesthesia was almost as extensive but far more moderate in English romanticism; and its use in English poetry was rather to give, as it were, an additional dimension to an image by bringing to bear the further interpretation of another sense. Thus, Keats may use such phrases as "embalmèd darkness," "shadows of melodious utterance," "the *touch* of *scent*," or "bowers of *fragrant* and enwreathèd *light*." Or he may make incense almost tangible by calling it "soft" and by picturing it as "hanging":

> I cannot see what flowers are at my feet
> Nor what *soft incense hangs* upon the boughs.

The poet, said Coleridge, must command "what Bacon calls the *vestigia communia* of the senses, the latency of all in each, and more especially as by a magical *penna duplex*, the excitement of vision by sound and the exponents of sound." Similarly, Hazlitt defined "gusto" as a powerful vitality of feeling which, when called forth, pervades and dominates the senses with a synthetic and unifying control: it is possessed by an artist when "the impressions made on one sense excite by affinity those of another"; and Hazlitt complained of Claude Lorraine's landscapes that "they do not interpret one sense by another . . . that is, his eye wanted imagination: it did not sympathize with his other faculties. He saw the atmosphere, but did not *feel* it." [12]

Synaesthesia, at least in England, was one of the many progeny of eighteenth-century British associationism. Sir Isaac Newton, at the beginning of the century, had attempted to coördinate mathematically the colors refracted by a prism with the notes of the octave. In France, not long after, Father Castel, who decided that there was nothing like carrying a matter to its logical conclusion, built his intriguing color-clavichord. Thus the note *do*, because of an intrinsic "majesty," was equated with blue; *re*,

[12] Hazlitt, "On Gusto," *Works* (ed. Howe, 1931–1934), IV, 78–79.

because of a rural, sprightly quality, with green; and *sol*, which he considered a warlike and angry note, with red. We are told that the persevering Castel even considered performing concerts of perfumes by means of a clavichord of scent-boxes. Shortly after the middle of the century, synaesthesia was treated with occasional seriousness in England. Locke had told of a blind man who likened scarlet to the sound of a trumpet. The story had since been often repeated as an illustration of the imagination's potentialities for error; but it was now sometimes quoted with commendation of the blind man's perspicacity! Several associationists began to discuss the emotional interrelation of sight, sound, and touch. A familiar example is Edmund Burke's inclusion of smoothness as one of the properties of the beautiful; for there is a "chain," he said, "in all our sensations; they are all but different sorts of *feelings* calculated . . . to be affected after the same manner."

Erasmus Darwin, following Newton's premises, almost thought that synaesthesia could be made into an exact science. Uvedale Price, again, who believed that Locke's blind man "had great reason to pride himself on his discovery," regarded "picturesqueness" in art as proof of the "general harmony and correspondence in all our sensations . . . though they affect us by means of different senses." The "picturesque" in painting is essentially distinguished by roughness and irregularity — qualities which are originally discerned by the sense of touch:

Besides the real irritation, which is produced by means of broken lights, all broken, rugged, and abrupt surfaces have also by sympathy somewhat of the same effect on the sight as on the touch. Indeed, as it is generally admitted that the sense of seeing acquires its perceptions of hard, soft, rough, smooth, &c., from that of feeling, such a sympathy seems almost unavoidable.

Even music, as in "a capricious movement of Scarlatti or Haydn," may occasionally be called "picturesque":

such a movement, from its sudden, unexpected, and abrupt tendencies,
— from a certain playful wildness of character and appearance of irregularity, is no less analogous to similar scenery in nature, than the concerto
or the chorus to what is grand or beautiful to the eye.[13]

Similarly, a gently sloping bank may suggest "the quality of
smoothness, and consequently of ease and repose to a person while
he is viewing it, just as it does when he afterwards sits or lies
down upon it." An example of such an inner "sympathy" of the
senses is Shakespeare's "How sweet the moonlight *sleeps* upon
this bank!" Nothing here specifically states what sort of bank it
was, said Price; "but if you fancy it broken and abrupt, the moon
might indeed *shine*, but it could no longer *sleep* upon it."

A perception, moreover, may not only produce an effect congruous with that of a perception by another sense, a congruity
which, because it is felt as a genuine response of human nature,
deserves portrayal in art; but it may also possess, as some of the
Shaftesburyans had earlier pointed out, an effect analogous to
that of a general disposition of mind or feeling. Thus Archibald
Alison, among others, found analogies between colors and certain emotions, and, because these analogies apparently exist for
the generality of mankind, he considered them natural rather
than accidental. Since white is usually associated with day, its
effect inclines to be one of "cheerfulness"; black, associated with
night, produces a reaction not dissimilar to "gloom or melancholy"; while blue, as the color of the heavens in serene weather,
"is expressive to us of somewhat the same pleasing and temperate
Character." An example of a merely "local" analogy, however,
would be purple, which "has acquired a character of Dignity
from its accidental connection with the dress of Kings." Analogies may also exist between "certain affections of the mind" and
the mere degree or intensity of a color: "Soft or Strong, Mild or

[13] Uvedale Price, *Essays on the Picturesque* (rev. ed., 1810), I, 46, 118–119,
160.

Bold, Gay or Gloomy . . . are terms in all languages applied
to Colours . . . and indicate their connection with particular
qualities of Mind."

This sort of speculation became something of a pastime among
many people. Even Hume was intrigued by it. On meeting the
blind poet, Thomas Blacklock, he was at once curious to know
Blacklock's feelings about certain colors. Hume then reported to
Joseph Spence, who was always interested in the reactions of an
"original genius," that "the Illumination of the Sun, for instance, he supposed to resemble the presence of a Friend; the
cheerful color of Green, to be like an amiable Sympathy, &c."
Moreover, "the constitution of our nature," said Alison, leads
us to perceive resemblances between emotions and sensations in
general, and consequently between the objects that produce them.
There is thus an analogy of sorts

between the Sensation of gradual Ascent, and the Emotion of Ambition,
— between the Sensation of gradual Descent, and the Emotion of Decay,
— between the lively Sensation of Sunshine, and the cheerful Emotion
of Joy, — between the painful Sensation of Darkness, and the dispiriting
Emotion of Sorrow. In the same manner, there are analogies between
Silence and Tranquillity, — between the lustre of Morning, and the
gaiety of Hope, — between softness of Colouring, and gentleness of
Character, — between slenderness of Form, and delicacy of Mind. . . .[14]

For example, slow "motion in Curves is expressive of Ease, of
Freedom, of Playfulness, and is consequently beautiful"; and, by
its association with curving motion, the perception of a serpentine
or winding line — Hogarth's famous "line of beauty" — may affect one exactly as does the state of "Volition and Ease," and
therefore be justifiably used to express that state. Or again, the
same "sublime" reaction may be elicited by the sight of great
elevation and the feeling of magnanimity, or by the conception of
great depth and the emotion of horror.

[14] Alison, *Essays on Taste* (Edinburgh: 1790), pp. 131–132.

VI

The emotions of man have common ground: the intensity set up by one provides easy access for the admission of a further emotion; and grief, love, anger, hate, and fear may all easily pass into each other. The border line between feelings, indeed, is so thin as to be almost hypothetical. The framework of the passions, as Hume had said,

is not like a wind instrument, which, in running over all the notes, immediately loses the sound when the breath ceases; but rather resembles a string-instrument, where, after each stroke, the vibrations still retain some sound. . . . Each stroke will not produce a clear and distinct note of passion, but the one passion will always be mixed . . . with the other.[15]

This conception of the interworking and interfluctuation, so to speak, of the passions was extended by several associationist critics; and one may note, in such extensions, an emergence of the romantic confidence that, whereas reason, in Schlegel's words, "can only comprise each object separately, . . . *Feeling* perceives all in all at one and the same time," and hence is susceptible to certain analogies which could not otherwise be descried. There seems to be a general assumption that, with one feeling inevitably exciting another by affinity, man's emotional nature is almost a kind of sounding board: that an impression may there give rise to a general reverberation, as it were, which will in turn, by a kind of reverse procedure, again find outward analogy and expression in other, externally different perceptions and inclinations. The development of this general premise would not only account for such ramifications as associational synaesthesia or as the subjectively felt analogies between sensations and emotions themselves; it would also be one of the contributing elements to the common romantic emphasis on "suggestiveness."

[15] Hume, "Dissertation on the Passions" (1757), *Works* (1854), IV, 191.

At least one aspect of the evolution of the conception of "sublimity" pertinently illustrates the progressive working towards "suggestiveness." The state of elevation or transport which Longinus had postulated as characteristic of the sublime was one which had as its end the insight into the ideal or the universal. Empiricism, with its confidence in sensation alone, quickly sanctioned a tendency to regard sublimity as simply an exhilaration which is evoked by contemplating what is large enough to challenge conception to its fullest exertion. The influence of Locke's sensationalism on Addison's conception of "greatness" is characteristic: by the sight of great magnitude, the imagination is "flung into a pleasing astonishment," and both mind and the emotions — since their condition is determined by their objects — are thus completely released from "restraint."

By the middle of the century, sublimity had become almost synonymous with the highest possible emotion which could be aroused. It was with this belief that Edmund Burke, in his famous work on *The Origin of Our Ideas of the Sublime and Beautiful* (1757), made terror a basis of sublimity; for whatever "operates in a manner analogous to terror . . . is productive of the strongest emotion which the mind is capable of feeling." A less frankly sensationalistic and certainly a less terror-ridden interpretation quickly ensued. Sublimity might be equated with "magnitude," "majesty," or "grandeur"; or more often, among the associationists, with anything which suggested "force" or "power." But in almost all cases the sublime, as one writer said, "dilates and expands the mind, and puts its grasp to trial"; and it is conceded to be that which displays — and demands from the beholder — the most vigorous response of imagination and feeling. Familiar illustrations of this sublime vigor are Homer, Shakespeare, Milton, and the Bible, especially the books of Isaiah and Job. A number of patriotic Scots, moreover, never failed to instance also Macpherson's Ossianic forgeries, which swept much of Europe and were dear to the heart of Napoleon, but which Reynolds cited as an example of the "false sublime" and Johnson thought could have been written by "many men, many women, and many children."

The frequent opposing of sublimity to the artificial, the sophisticated, and the weakly regular may be exemplified by such works as William Duff's *Essay on Original Genius* (1767). "The sublime," said Duff, "is the proper walk of a great Genius, in which it delights to range, and in which alone it can display its powers to advantage, or put forth its strength." Any emotion which is capable of attaining genuine elevation partakes of sublimity when it is sufficiently intense and searching; hence writers from Duff to Knight stressed the intimate connection between the sublime and the pathetic; and Knight added that, when felt with enough vitality, all sympathetic identification is sublime. But "it is one thing," as Burke said, "to make an image clear, and another to make it affecting to the imagination"; and whatever may constitute sublimity, it is always strongly favored by a certain amount of "obscurity." "We yield to sympathy," added Burke, "what we refuse to description." In Homer's one opening line about the wrath of Achilles, said Ogilvie, he suggests a "hero unbridled, furious, implacable, resentful"; but in the *Aeneid*, Virgil "opens his subject with a detail of circumstances which . . . strike not the mind so forcibly when taken together as the single stroke of his inimitable rival."

For the vitality and vigor with which the sublime is felt arises less from sensation than from an energetically subjective activity of the mind; and whatever "increases this exercise or employment of Imagination," stated Alison, "increases also the *emotion* of beauty or sublimity." The unstated and indefinite encourages this exercise. A thunderstorm, continued Alison, is customarily considered sublime; "but there is a low and feeble sound which precedes it, more sublime in reality than all the uproar of the storm itself." The premonition of what is to come, either in nature or in a work of art, tempts a creative and independent reaction from the observer, reader, or hearer: it incites a deeper tension, in which are concentrated and resolved all felt anticipations and images which he can associate with what is to follow. It is largely because it excites a more energetic response of imagination and feeling that the sublime is profounder in effect than the beautiful. For art can most successfully elicit feeling and secure a consequent sympathetic understanding only when, disregarding entrance by piecemeal perception of detail, it penetrates at once to the emotional frame, and, arousing there "a strong working of mind," as Coleridge later said, effects a complete "substitution of a sublime *feeling* of the unimaginable for a mere image."

VII

Suggestiveness also becomes a necessary means in proportion to the degree that an aesthetic object is employed for "expression" rather than "*im*pression." For expression strives, through suggestion, to disclose what is beyond the formal quality of the object. It thus transcends the limitations of what could at any one time be known through an intrinsic presentation; and by doing so, it achieves a superior scope and variety, and a more multiform plexus of potential meaning. Its use in humanistic classicism is less pronounced, and is also channeled towards a determined end: the suggestion, for example, in classical sculpture, of a potential readiness for all possible rounded and liberal activities is a suggestion which is always subdued to an ideal decorum and consonance; and its implication of the universal is combined with an almost imposed clarity of purpose and form. The romantic employment of expression is more restless: it reveals a decreased confidence in the intrinsic value of immediate aesthetic form; and it seeks less to declare the harmony and order of the determined or the given than to awaken an inference or feeling of the undetermined or the undeclared. In its attempt to evoke inference rather than to impose form, and thus to appeal directly to the individual associations or feelings of the beholder, romantic suggestiveness had several later ramifications, which might vary from the occasional nineteenth-century cult of "magic" and "wonder" — the romantic period, said Theodore Watts-Dunton, was "the renascence of wonder" — to the hardly less subjective but highly intellectualized symbolism which somewhat succeeded it. As it is most successfully present in English romanticism, however, the use of suggestion, though primarily emotional and even subjective in its effect, tended to be centripetal instead of extreme or deliberate.

In addition to the greater number of ideas and of nuances of feeling which suggestiveness, by going beyond the object, can excite, the very activity of mind which is aroused is one of the primary satisfactions which art can give. "Nothing more powerfully excites any affection," Hume had stated, "than to conceal some part of its object, by throwing it into a kind of shade, which, at the same time that it shows enough to prepossess us in favor of the object, leaves still some work for the imagination." Critics of the later eighteenth century frequently insisted that resemblance must never be too exact in art. Much of aesthetic pleasure, said Adam Smith, is determined by the very "degree of disparity between the imitating and the imitated object": imitation fruits and flowers, for example, please far less than a mere picture of them, and painted statues have less appeal than unpainted ones. By summoning up an active response of imagination and feeling, moreover, an augmented vitality of realization is made possible. Erasmus Darwin, speaking of the importance of suggestiveness, mentioned a sketch of "a shrivelled hand stretched through an iron grate in the stone floor of a prison-yard, to reach at a mess of porrage, which affected me with more horrid ideas of the distress of the prisoner in the dungeon below than could have been perhaps produced by an exhibition of the whole person." [16]

Similarly, in poetry, metaphors must not be too close, nor descriptions too detailed. Darwin cited the brief, pathetic statement

[16] Darwin, *Botanic Garden* (1789–1791), II, 125–126.

of Lear: "Pray you, undo this button. Thank you, Sir." Here the "oppression at the bosom of the dying King is made visible, not described in words." By the use of "the language of suggestion," wrote Richard Edgeworth, "Agamemnon hiding his face at the sacrifice of his daughter expresses little to the eye, but much to the imagination." Or in the line, "Springs upward like a Pyramid of fire," Milton, said Beattie, evokes a conception, all at one instant, both of Satan's enormous size and refulgent appearance and of motion so swift "as to appear a continued track of light, and lessening to the view according to the increase of distance, till it end in a point, and then disappear."

Indeed, because of its capacity for immediate penetration, poetry is often stressed by some of the later associationists as superior to the visual arts. "The Painter addresses himself to the Eye," said Alison; "the Poet speaks to the Imagination"; and the statement was something of a commonplace by the end of the century. The "presence of genius," Coleridge later maintained, is not shown by

elaborating a picture: we have had many specimens of this sort of work in modern poems, where all is so dutchified, if I may use the word, by the most minute touches, that the reader naturally asks why words, and not painting, are used. . . . The power of poetry is, by a single word, perhaps, *to instil energy into the mind, which compels the imagination to produce the picture*. Prospero tells Miranda,

> One midnight,
> Fated to the purpose, did Antonio open
> The gates of Milan; and i' the dead of darkness,
> The ministers for the purpose hurried thence
> Me, and thy *crying* self.

Here, by introducing a single happy epithet, "crying," . . . a complete picture is presented to the mind, and in the production of such pictures the power of genius consists.[17]

---

[17] Coleridge, *Shakespearean Criticism* (ed. Raysor, Cambridge, Mass.: 1930), II, 174.

For man's inner reservoir of feeling, perpetually animated by the ready creative impulse of the imagination, responds, when given a suggestive fillip, with a faithful re-creation of its own which is more vitally appreciated and more sympathetically comprehended than any merely passive and externally noted observation could be. And, in its act of re-creation, it achieves an intensity of conception from which the extraneous and the discordant "evaporate," and which is therefore able to divine certain relations, qualities, and energies hitherto unapparent. "The excellence of every art," said Keats, "is its intensity, capable of making all disagreeables evaporate from their being in close relationship with Beauty and Truth." In the unity of creative insight which this intensity produces, the complete meaning and character of its object stand revealed as a sudden "swelling into reality" — a reality, Keats said, which is "all ye know on earth," and which, because it is the true, the vital, the significant, is also seen as the beautiful.

CHAPTER VI.

THE ENGLISH ROMANTIC COMPROMISE

In the former part of the last century [wrote an admirer of rural life in 1803], it was usual with writers on moral subjects to insist much on the reason and fitness of things, their several natures and mutual relations . . . and to have deserted these grounds for the sake of a theory which leaves everyone to resolve his duty by his *feelings*, would have been thought at best extremely unphilosophical. How different are the times in which we live! [1]

The two preceding chapters attempted to point out that, as the eighteenth century progressed, the inevitable mechanistic and emotional reactions to neo-classic rationalism, as well as to what remained of classical and Renaissance humanism, received effective and consistent support from British empirical psychology. The closing years of the century were accordingly characterized by a general conviction decidedly different from that which it had inherited: a conviction that the essential nature of man was not reason — whether it be the ethical insight into the ideal or even the sheer mathematicism of the Cartesians — but that it consisted, in effect, either of a conglomeration of instincts, habits, and feelings, or else, as German subjectivism was beginning to illustrate, of an ego which creates and projects its own world, and which has little real hope of knowing anything else. There are frequent indications of a restless and at times startled awareness of the newly-discovered inadequacy of man's mind and knowledge — an awareness which somewhat stimulated and also

[1] Ely Bates, *Rural Philosophy: or Reflections on Knowledge, Virtue, and Happiness* (1803), pref. p. vii.

received temporary balm from man's increasing scientific conquest of external nature.⌋ A more widespread temptation was to glorify at least one aspect of the discovery: to find the sole attainable validity and worth either in one form or another of sentiment or else in some other essentially non-rational capacity.

This glorification, however diverse in its aspects, is one of the most distinguishing characteristics of the romanticism which the later eighteenth century formulated and bequeathed to Western Europe. Examples are both numerous and extremely familiar. We may recall the widespread wave of primitivism which took rise at this time, and which Johnson continually combated: the confidence — so familiarly exemplified by Rousseau — that the "natural" man is good, and that, once his fetters are removed, he will inevitably fulfill himself and reattain the Golden Age. This confidence in the "natural" man was many-sided in its effects and manifestations. It was partly humanitarian and political, and its influence on the French Revolution, of course, is a byword. It also encouraged the common romantic emphasis on the virtues of simple and rural life, and, in its extremer form, as Mr. Fairchild has shown, found outlet in continuing the cult of the "noble savage" who is unspoiled by contact with civilization. It lent a kind of sanction to the vogue of the untutored and "original genius"; and the frequent dilating on the "natural" innocence and goodness of childhood is an equally common expression of it.

A trust in natural sentiment and inclination was not only primitivistic: it also gave a heartening impetus to the conception of progress which retained so marked a prominence throughout the whole nineteenth century. Few books have ever achieved so quick if temporary a vogue as William Godwin's *Political Justice* (1793), where the basic equality of all men's innate goodness is urged in conjunction with the theory of "perfectibility." In 1800, said Hazlitt twenty-five years later, Godwin "was in the very zenith of a sultry and unwholesome popularity . . . no one was more talked of, more sought after, and wherever liberty, truth, and justice was the theme, his name was not far off. . . . Tom Paine was for the time considered as Tom Fool to him, Paley an old woman, and Edmund Burke a flashy sophist." "Throw away your books of Chemistry," said the younger Wordsworth to a student, "and read Godwin"; and Shelley and others were not slow in taking heed. It is significant that, although Godwin at first considered himself a "rationalist," he was really very much in the English benevolist tradition; that he adopted Hume's principle of sympathy; and that he planned ultimately to rewrite his *Political Justice*, and found his system upon "feeling." This combination of the belief in natural goodness and in progress was to some extent drawn upon by British utilitarianism — with its creed of "the greatest happiness of the greatest number" — and may be illustrated in its popular form by such works as Mary Hays' novel, *Emma Courtney* (1796), where the heroine makes it her goal to facilitate progress and to work "towards the great end of life — *general utility*." In France, where so many English tendencies have been carried to their logical extremes, the fruition of one aspect of romantic utilitarianism was soon typified by the positivist sociolatry of Auguste Comte. Since "nothing is absolute, but all is relative" — a statement he never tired of repeating — Comte, like the French mechanist, Du Marsais, concluded that "Society is the only Divinity," and preached a "religion of humanity." This religion he later elaborated under the "angelic influence" of Mme Clotilde de Vaux, without which, as he modestly said, he would have been merely another Aristotle. The uncharitable may find a warning, as did M. Gilson, in the list of books which Comte made out for the "Positivist Library": such men as Plato, Spinoza, and Leibniz are omitted, whereas some of the British empiricists are present side by side with Mme de Lambert's *Counsels of a Mother*. "Hume," said Comte, "is my principal predecessor in philosophy." We may remember that, when Hume considered the possible consequences of his philosophy, he was "affrighted and confounded."

Though it attempted to combat both empiricism and emotional relativism, contemporary German thought stemmed from the same source and revealed some of the same general characteristics which attended upon other aspects of subjectivism. Having proved that reality is forever unknowable to the intellect, Kant was forced to find a non-rational means for feeling or manifesting, if not actually knowing, the good; and this he discovered in the "will." Kant was keenly aware of possible misinterpretations, and continually qualified himself. It was left for his truant pupil, Fichte, to conclude that nature itself is only the creation of the ego — or the will — which is in turn the product and manifestation of the "Eternal and Infinite Will": "Thou and I," said Fichte to the "Infinite Will," "are not divided! Thy voice sounds within me; mine resounds in Thee!" And after the close of the eighteenth century, Hegel, attempting to find a unity and direction which would transcend individual subjectivism, preached that truth is the "realization or actualization of the Whole," and that in any form of "individuality" there is a "negation" involved. But being a relativist — at least in the classical sense — he could find no real "whole," for all moral intents and purposes, beyond that of the state; and with the progressive welfare of the state thus constituting "the onward march of God," it is perhaps inevitable that he should have added that "the military class is the class of universality." "Had there been no Rousseau," said Napoleon, "there would have been no Revolution; had there been no Revolution, *I* should have been impossible."

The recollection of such broad tendencies as the few which have been mentioned here is perhaps necessary in any general consideration of romanticism. They may serve to remind us of the extent, the pervasiveness, and the variety of the anti-rationalistic movement of which romanticism reflects or comprises the first stage. They may also remind us of the problems that begin to confront any system of values, whether ethical or aesthetic, which abandons a rational conception of the objective good as the distinctive characteristic of man. If something in man, such as emotion or the will, is postulated as independent of reason or as transcending it in attaining the good, the question then arises what the good is and how it is possibly to be known. And the answer is too often one which either begs the question or else cites a purely empirical or utilitarian end. Even Friedrich Schlegel noted that, since Hume, "nothing more has been attempted than merely to erect all sorts of barriers against the *practical* influence of this destructive tendency"; and this attempt to divert or glorify certain effects of relativism rather than to strike at its source has resulted, he adds, either in making social and "national welfare the ruling principle of thought" — a principle "quite unfitted to be the center and oracle of *all* knowledge and science" — or else in relying upon "moral feeling and on sympathy," which, since individual predilection diverges boundlessly, "are too frail and uncertain for a rule of moral action." The continued application of either result necessitates a sanguine belief in a progress inherent in man's natural and even subjective self or else in the general empirical scheme of things. The gradual evaporation of this belief was mirrored in art, as the nineteenth century wore to a close, by a decay and growing aimlessness in romanticism and by a subsequent transition to a barer, more searching, and occasionally a more naturalistic relativism.

Owing to an array of extraordinary individual talent, the early nineteenth century, especially in music and literature, takes rank among the greatest periods of western art; and few generalizations consistently apply to the outstanding exponents of romanticism. Yet because it did not exist in an aesthetic vacuum but was so closely interrelated with a general relativistic subjectivism, romantic art has been frequently censured during the twentieth century, and perhaps with some justice. It may certainly be admitted that if art is to emancipate and give voice to the subjective associations and feelings of the individual, it is difficult to draw the line between what is valid and what is not. The ultimate temptation is to abandon a line of demarcation. Criticism, in that case, assumes an "expressionist" point of view, like that of Croce: it merely inquires what the artist's intention was and how well he succeeded; and it neglects a third question, upon which Goethe was careful to insist: what is the worth of the artist's intention? Moreover, "a subjective nature," as he remarked, "has soon talked out his little internal material, and is at last ruined by mannerism. . . . I call the classic *healthy*, and the romantic *sickly*." Wordsworth himself was aware that his "associations must have sometimes been particular instead of general, and that consequently, giving to things a false importance, I may sometimes have written on unworthy subjects." We may also admit that self-expression too often results, as Irving Babbitt pointed out, in a corruption of the Aristotelean *katharsis* — a degeneration into the *katharsis* which a recent critic exalts as the same "grateful feeling . . . a hen achieves every time she lays an egg": "I am aware," said Rousseau, "that the reader need not know these details, but I need to tell him." The accompanying self-absorption which is sometimes found in extreme romanticism had various ramifications. As distinct from that of more recent art, it was often marked by the sort of sensibility of which Hazlitt complained in Rousseau: "His alternate pleasures and pains are the bead-roll that he tells over and piously worships." Furthermore, the common romantic conception of the spontaneous "unconsciousness" of genius — as it was urged, that is, by its more extreme spokesmen — admittedly bears affinities with the hasty and primitivistic opposition between the "natural" and the "artificial." On the continent, its interrelation with the general extolling of mere expansiveness was extremely pronounced — as Babbitt, again, has amusingly if at times unfairly shown — in the French Rousseauists and in the German *Sturm und Drang*; and we may remember Fichte's praise of the Germans as an *Urfolk* in whom the natural and the unconscious spontaneously wells up. Similarly, at least some of the "communion" with nature — though not that of Wordsworth, yet that of many lesser figures — was undeniably a mere communion with one's own mood. An awareness of this was perhaps one of the sources of romantic melancholy. Though they might at times believe that "Nature never did betray that heart that loves her," some romanticists realized only too well that they "pined for what is not." But the matter can easily be pushed too far. It was admittedly in an *Ode on Dejection*, for example, that Coleridge wrote "in *our* life alone doth Nature live"; but the "shaping spirit of imagination" which, for Coleridge, illuminates the "inanimate cold world" could be confused with "mood" or an outrush of sentiment only by the most determined anti-romantic.

II

Indeed, recent censuring of the subjective element in romanticism, both by critics who have merely substituted another and less effusive form of individualism and by writers who have condemned all forms of modern relativistic subjectivism, has suffered from the quick generalization which tempts any judgment by one age of another immediately preceding it. Much adverse criticism is particularly vulnerable to the charge of indiscrimination in its view of the strictly aesthetic aims and qualities of early nineteenth-century romanticism. There has especially been an occasional but blatant failure to distinguish between, on the one hand, the spontaneity and emotional intensity which are prized — and attained — in romantic criticism and art, and, on the other hand, the expansive egocentricity and aimless sentimentality of which it is only too easy to find indications throughout the later eighteenth and entire nineteenth centuries.

The romantic use of suggestion, to take but one instance, may be condemned as capable of becoming indeterminate and limp: of evoking merely such random recollections and images as are

already near the surface; of inducing a revery or a kind of
Paterian "stirring of the senses," which may "set the spirit free
for a moment" but which admittedly leaves it undisciplined, unsettled, and without purpose. That this has encouraged an occasional cultivation of nostalgia for its own sake is a familiar and
indeed valid charge. But it is a charge which has been hastily
and indiscriminately flung about, especially by the followers of
Irving Babbitt, who felt that even a little yearning was a dangerous thing. For, except during the later seventeenth and early
eighteenth centuries, a use of suggestion far transcending that in
classical antiquity had been intrinsic and traditional in much
European art and literature, particularly in the individualization
of emotions which flowered in one aspect of the baroque and in
the early seventeenth-century interest in the dramatic. Instances
had abounded, not least of all in Shakespeare, Milton, and Rembrandt, of its indispensability in prompting imaginative reach and
a vitality of inference; and these instances may be especially
paralleled by recourse to much of the English poetry of the
romantic movement. Similarly, the more felicitous attempts of
romantic poetry to reveal analogies and significances which exist
to subjective reaction alone rarely transgressed the limits which
English criticism had marked out during the second half of the
eighteenth century; and as such they should be sharply distinguished from the marked subjectivity of less happy and later
efforts of romanticism. Even in the much-ridiculed interest in
"synaesthesia," there is a difference between the moderate and
legitimate speculations of the eighteenth-century associationists, of
Hazlitt, or of Coleridge, and the more extreme and self-indulging
notions of Rousseau and Diderot; between Keats's masterly use
of several senses in strengthening an image and the sort of thing
later exemplified by Rimbaud's comparison of the five vowels to
various colors, by the aesthete of the nineties who wished to "say
mad scarlet things and awaken the night with silver silences,"
or by the hero of Huysmans's novel, *A Rebours,* who devotes

himself to composing concerts of perfumes and liqueurs, and who at length collapses in the arms of a nerve-specialist.

Critics who rather too arbitrarily oppose the classic and the romantic as diametrical opposites often take pause to caution us not to judge the various ramifications of classicism by what they degenerated into; yet the same critics, in upbraiding European romanticism, have cited as illustration and tended to think in terms of the several extremes into which romanticism was capable of degenerating. To say, for example, that the stylistic premises and values of such writers as Wordsworth, Hazlitt, or Keats were admissions inevitably leading to the diffuse "dampness" which often characterizes poorer romantic art and criticism, and which seems to repel many critics of the present day, is almost as weak a generalization as to say that in Aristotle are the inevitable seeds of Thomas Rymer; and if one judges by potential degeneration in both instances, the question seems to subside into whether one is more averse to a marsh than a desert.

In common with much other nineteenth and twentieth-century art, many of even the most successful examples of romanticism admittedly lack a certain moral centrality which is familiar in so much classical, Renaissance, and even neo-classic art. But the various styles of the most successful romantic art were at least guided by purposes which transcend the mere exploitation of emotional mood or technical interest. It should be noted, indeed, that a romanticization of subject matter long precedes the deliberate romanticization of the aesthetic medium. The poems of Goldsmith are characteristic in this respect; and even through the *Lyrical Ballads* (1798) of Wordsworth and Coleridge, and the narrative poems of Scott, Byron, and Keats, an almost orthodox interest in action and event is still retained, and the romantic themes tend to dictate the imagery, the vocabulary, and even the versification. In the *Lyrical Ballads*, said Wordsworth, "each of these poems has a purpose . . . the feeling therein developed gives importance to the action and situation, and not the action and situation to the feeling"; and, although the statement — as Hazlitt pointed out — is not strictly true, its intention, at least, is significant. A contrast is thus offered to the later poetry of the nineteenth century, where, as notoriously in Swinburne's poems on classical themes, subjects are assumed of any sort, and are then employed as a mere backdrop to the conscious romanticization of style *per se*. In Victorian poetry, the past, for example, is frequently reverted to not because it offers romantic subjects but because of what it can offer associationally to the diction and the imagery: because the very nostalgia evoked by it furnishes an easy and immediate emotional response which would permit a stylistic manipulation and development of mood. The poetic aestheticism of this period gave additional opportunity to the development of the novel as one of the few remaining *genres* which could still have pertinence to life.

A parallel is to be observed in the evolution of nineteenth-century painting. Whereas Michelangelo had sought to idealize the human being, and Rembrandt to portray him as he is, early nineteenth-century painting romanticized its subject matter. But the delineation of object, action, or scene was still a basic concern. It remained for the latter half of the century to busy itself primarily with problems of light and shade, of color, and of form as ends in themselves; and the parallel with the music of that period and with its interest in tonal coloring is even more pronounced. Many twentieth-century reactions to this tendency were reactions against languor, insipidity, or exhausted conventions, but constituted no break in fundamental direction; and the subjectivistic concern with the aesthetic medium itself, either for its emotional and associational potentialities or for a somewhat more formalistic conception of technique, not only remained but became almost scientific.

The moderation in the general stylistic character of romantic art at its best is also to be attributed to its ability to profit from tradition without becoming eclectic and reminiscent. The comparative restraint of English romanticism, in particular, was partly due to an acute if occasionally confined awareness of English poetic tradition. And, more than any other European people, the English possessed a large body of creative literature which had been written before neo-classic rationalism became extensively reflected in European art; and this literature, in addition to its other attributes, had been characterized by an imaginative strength and an emotional spontaneity which were at once congenial to romanticism and which at the same time had been channeled to either a religious, formal, or objectively dramatic end.

The subjectivistic assumptions of romantic criticism itself, however, have perhaps been more vulnerable. Throughout the eighteenth century, British empirical and psychological criticism had increasingly created a temptation to regard the beautiful as a by-product of the mind's subjective working rather than as the selective "imitation" of an idealized nature. It therefore sought to analyze the character of the reactions which make up both taste and aesthetic creation before it pronounced upon art. It is somewhat in this vein that Coleridge insisted that the poet's aim is less to "copy nature" than to "create forms according to the severe laws of the intellect"; and he consequently attempted, as he said, "to ground my opinions in the component faculties of the human mind itself, and their comparative dignity and importance. According to the faculty or source, from which the pleasure given by any poem or passage was derived, I estimated the merit of such poem or passage." The crystallization of this tendency is pre-eminently exemplified on the continent, of course, by Kant: any estimate of the beautiful, said Kant, must be based upon the analysis of the aesthetic sense or taste; and the determinations of taste "can be no other than subjective." The conception of art as a kind of excrescence of mind rather than as an imitation of significant objective reality was, like other legacies of eighteenth-century British empiricism, extremely profitable to particularized aesthetic criticism; but as a basic conception it was in some respects a potential Trojan Horse, and one, it may be noted, which was hardly the sort that the Greeks would have bestowed. Less happy possibilities accrued in proportion as the mind was seen to be increasingly restricted in its communication with the external world; for the assumption that the reactions of the subjective mind are the only certain phenomena is one which may lead to almost any eventuality. The methods of meeting this problem were multifarious; they became more so as the nineteenth century progressed, and have varied from an almost complete relativism to attempted ramifications of Schiller's and Schelling's "objective idealism" and of the Kantian doctrine of "the universal subjective validity of taste."

Yet many of the generalizations which may be made about the basic character of romantic aesthetic theory are as little applicable to the more sober criticism of this period as they would be to that of any other. For major romantic critics were far from prepared to accept all the extreme consequences of the problem of subjective taste. As in the notable examples of Goethe and Hazlitt, they occasionally turned back to classical antiquity and especially the Renaissance; they turned directly, that is, to art itself, as it flourished in its greatest epochs, and sought to derive their standards from it; nor should it be forgotten that, among the severest judges of this period, were men who themselves dwelt in it. The general stream of lesser romantic criticism also refused at last to follow the exclusive lead of psychological speculation, but with less success; and by the middle of the nineteenth century, aesthetics and criticism became effectively divorced and traveled in substantially the same direction but by very different roads. The English in particular, having virtually created the modern science of aesthetics, or having at least established the subjective basis from which aesthetics was to proceed, in general refused to become professional aestheticians, and abandoned the subject to the academic dialectic and later the pragmatic experimentation of the German universities. They themselves turned either to the favorite and often suggestively fruitful English pastime of appreciative description or else to the historical study of their own literature and of the classics; and a Victorian or Edwardian critic of philosophical inclination became almost as rare as an aesthetician who possessed an extensive knowledge of art or any genuine susceptibility to it.

III

Despite its strong empirical bent, English criticism especially tended to avoid excessive subjectivism during the early nineteenth century. Subjectivism in one form or another is perhaps an inevitable companion of extreme empiricism. But the British confidence in the teaching of experience at least prevented an acceptance, by the more sober, either of "natural" feeling and inclination as a guide or of the elaborate subjectivistic systems which were being worked out in Germany; indeed, Hazlitt's reaction to the first of these two tendencies — and Hazlitt, in his fundamental premises, is perhaps the most representative English critic of the period — was one of strong and often clear-sighted antagonism.

It has been one of the purposes of the two preceding chapters to show that, as these terms were evolved in later eighteenth-century British criticism, "imagination" is hardly to be confused with revery or rank illusion, and that "feeling" is seldom to be regarded as equivalent to "impulse." Such terms — like any others — were admittedly capable of the loosest connotation, and, in popular moral and semi-critical writing, sometimes bore a marked Rousseauistic coloring. But most early-nineteenth-century critics of any significance continued to use them as means of implying a broader and more intense awareness and employment of experience than can be achieved by analytical enumeration or by the artificial postulation of separate categories and concepts. In its unification, for example, of all varieties of mental exercise and response, eighteenth-century associationism had occasionally tended to designate them all, in a loose way, as "feelings": thus sensations, as Hartley said, are those "internal feelings of the mind which are produced by sense-impressions," whereas "all of our other internal feelings may be called ideas." Indeed, as Hugh Blair had said, though with a different implication, the divergence

between the authors who found the standard of taste upon the common feelings of human nature ascertained by general approbation, and those who found it upon established principles which can be ascertained by reason, is more an apparent than a real difference. Like many other controversies, it turns chiefly upon modes of expression.[2]

The use of the word "feeling" in this sense survived well into the nineteenth century, and may be characteristically exemplified by the Scottish intuitionist, Thomas Brown, whose works comprise one of the most detailed and descriptive syntheses of the joint associationist-intuitionist tendency. To Brown, all intellection is distinguished by "feelings of relation" and also by a central "desire" — by a purpose, interest, or concern, that is. This dominant and controlling "desire,"

like every other vivid feeling, . . . [according to] its permanence, tends to keep the accompanying conception of the subject, which is the object of the desire, also permanent before us; and while it is thus permanent, the usual spontaneous suggestions [i.e., associations] take place; conception following conception, in rapid but relative series. . . .[3]

It is this "desire" or interest, "co-existing with successive *feelings of relation* as they arise . . . to which we commonly give the name of reasoning." In addition to innate capacity, therefore, experience is obviously necessary: it broadens and even creates desire or interest, and it feeds and disciplines the associations by which "feelings of relation" arise. "Taste" is simply the application of this combinatory function of mind to the aesthetic realm:

[2] Hugh Blair, *Lectures on Rhetoric and Belles-Lettres* (1783), I, 32n.
[3] Thomas Brown, *Lectures on the Philosophy of the Human Mind* (Edinburgh: 1820), II, 398.

it presupposes, first, an "emotion" which is directed to an end, and which reacts in proportion to the significance of that end, whether it be an ideal, a design of action, a disclosure of character, or the self-sufficient form of a simple object; but it also includes a sensitive "feeling of the relations of fitness" towards that end — a feeling schooled by an extensive acquaintance not only with the specific medium of art but with all facets of life which can come within the province of art.

Similarly, Wordsworth tended to apply the term "feeling" to a state of comparatively vivid awareness, and "thought" to a later and vestigial "representative" of that awareness. It is necessary that the feeling be intense if the subsequent thought is to have pertinence and substance; "deep thinking," said Coleridge, "is attainable only by a man of deep feeling." It is with this implication of the word that, in terms and outlines which were later echoed and modified by Keats, Wordsworth took such pains to describe the evolution of the thinking mind. Thus, "boyhood" is a period of "glad animal movement" and of thoughtless and chaotic sensation; "youth," if sufficient native endowment is present, is characterized by intense feeling of various sorts which is not necessarily translated into thought; and, with the attainment of "maturity," the immediate delight in sensation disappears, while feeling continues but culminates in thought — "feelings," said Coleridge, "die by flowing into the mould of the intellect, becoming ideas." It should be noted parenthetically that an absorption in external nature was far from Wordsworth's intention. It was only in his youth that he "had a world about me . . . I made it, for it only lived to me"; and this was a period of mere "fancy," when "Imagination slept." In maturity, he said in the *Intimations of Immortality*,

> What though the radiance which was once so bright
> Be now forever taken from my sight,
> Though nothing can bring back the hour
> Of splendour in the grass, of glory in the flower;

We will grieve not, rather find
Strength in what remains behind;

.   .   .

In years that bring the philosophic mind.

The genuine philosophic mind, then, presupposes and necessitates feeling, particularly in youth. Art of any excellence, said Wordsworth, is produced only "by a man who, being possessed of more than usual organic sensibility, had also thought long and deeply. For our continued influxes of feeling are modified and directed by our thoughts, which are indeed the representatives of all our past feelings." [4]

"Without passion," as Hume had said, "no idea has any force." Similarly, taste — although it includes "a judgment that cannot be duped into admiration by aught that is unworthy for it" — must rest, added Wordsworth, upon "a natural sensibility that has been tutored into correctness without losing any of its quickness"; and those critics alone are to be heeded "who, never having suffered their youthful love of poetry to remit much of its force, have applied to the consideration of the laws of this art the best power of their understandings." The control of learning and experience by such a sensibility may hardly be regarded as the mere following of impulse, and, as Dugald Stewart said, actually prevents an aimless subservience or inclination to the temporary:

A sensibility, deep and permanent, to those objects of affection, admiration, and reverence, which interested the youthful heart . . . gives rise to the habits of attentive observation by which such a Taste alone can be formed; and it is this also that, binding and perpetuating the associations which such a Taste supposes, fortifies the mind against the fleeting caprices which the votaries of fashion watch and obey. [5]

[4] William Wordsworth, Preface to the *Lyrical Ballads, Prose Works* (ed. Grosart, 1876), II, 82.
[5] Dugald Stewart, "On Taste," *Philosophical Essays* (Edinburgh: 1810), pp. 470–471.

Since thought is a kind of conceptualization or abstraction from more immediate and vital experiences, "feeling" may thus be postulated as the groundwork of taste. But it also characterizes taste in an even·more inclusive sense. For coalesced "aggregates of simple ideas by association" in time tend themselves, as Hartley said, to form an "emotion." Ideas, evolved from primary or primitive feelings, may in turn pass into conceptions which, though broadened and rendered more valid after this intermediary process of abstraction, may be sufficiently unified and vivid in their appearance to deserve the designation of "feelings." It is in this respect that Wordsworth defined poetry as "the spontaneous overflow of powerful feelings" — of feelings which have been previously screened, as it were, by the process of thought; and poetry thus

take its origin from emotion recollected in tranquillity: the emotion is contemplated till, by a species of re-action, the tranquillity gradually disappears, and an emotion, kindred to that which was before the subject of contemplation, is gradually produced, and does itself actually exist in the mind.[6]

IV

Wordsworth's definition of the poetic process manifests a loose but very British assumption, and one which is rather prevalent in English romantic criticism, that "ideas" in general, when held with any intensity, can coalesce into almost emotional convictions. Thus sympathy, as Hume had stated, "is nothing but the conversion of an idea into an impression by the force of the imagination"; and this impression, when felt with sufficient vivacity, is in turn fused and transformed into the emotion which was originally observed in another human being. According to such a process, perceptions and ideas are capable of becoming melted, so to speak, into this crucible of imaginative and emotional response. Hazlitt's *Principles of Human Action* (1805), which probably had a strong influence

[6] Wordsworth, *Prose Works*, II, 96.

on Keats, especially exemplifies this assumption. The theme of the book, which is an argument against the Hobbist doctrine of innate self-love as the dominant principle of human action, is the formative adaptability of man's emotional character, and the complete dependence of the will upon whatever may be said to constitute mind. These principles are of course far from unclassical; they are among the primary suppositions of classicism. The mind inclines to that of which it possesses the most vivid idea; self-love is an effect rather than a cause, and arises when the individual has a clearer and more vivid idea, through direct experience, of his own "identity" than of the identities of others. But if the imagination is sufficiently wide and intense in its working, he may attain an equally clear and vigorous idea of the "identity" of another — an idea which, according as it is supported by intelligent and attentive observation, becomes transmuted into a sympathetic feeling of proportionate justness, and results in a consequent moral concern as strong as self-love, if not stronger.

This assumption that ideas can be resolved, converted, or as it were energized into persuasions and responses which are instantaneous in their working, and which thus deserve to be called "feelings," manifests — like the prevalent conception of the imagination in the English criticism of the period — a common conviction of British associationism and intuitionalism generally: the conviction, which was discussed in a previous chapter, that instinct of whatever sort feeds upon experience, and digests into its own automatic working the accumulated results of past impressions, reactions, thoughts, and judgments, however subtle or minute they may be when considered separately. Conceptions "may exist together," said Thomas Brown, "forming one complex feeling": each of the several parts of this feeling may branch out with endless associational tentacles, as it were; but, by means of a guiding emotional centrality, still be united in "one harmonizing whole"; and an appropriate use of "suggestion" in art will elicit these connected and relevant associations, not in piecemeal succession, but, under the control of a central feeling, in such a way that they "multiply and mingle as they arise."

In this awareness, the most fluid and elusive interrelations will be sensed; and, in the aesthetic realm especially, a truth and significance will be observed through all "the innumerable compositions and decompositions" — as Keats wrote — "which take place between the intellect and its thousand materials before it arrives at that trembling, delicate and snail-horn perception of beauty." And such an insight, with its grasp of the unique and organic totality of a phenomenon, will stand opposed to that artificial and abstracting faculty by which, as Wordsworth said in the *Prelude*, we

> pore, and dwindle as we pore,
> Viewing all objects unremittingly
> In disconnection dead and spiritless.

It is because of the spontaneity of its function, said Dugald Stewart, that taste is sometimes mistakenly assumed to be a simple sentiment; for "the transition from a Taste for the beautiful to that more comprehensive Taste," which extends its scope to all the several aspects of an art, is easy and gradual, and is characterized by an "insensible swelling in dimension." A familiar ramification of this attitude in Victorian criticism, though more restrictedly stylistic in its object, is found in Matthew Arnold's insistence that, in order to discern poetic excellence, one should have assimilated "lines and expressions of the great masters," and employ them as a kind of "touchstone" to other poetry:

Of course we are not to require this other poetry to resemble them; it may be very dissimilar. But if we have any tact we shall find them, when we have lodged them well in our minds, an infallible touchstone for detecting the presence or absence of high poetic quality, and also the degree of this quality . . .[7]

[7] Matthew Arnold, "Study of Poetry," *Essays in Criticism, Second Series* (1896), pp. 16–17.

Such an extended and trained fusion of feelings, then, is far from being confused by English romantic criticism with mere native "impulse"; and it is characteristic that Hazlitt, who profoundly distrusted "natural" inclination of the primitivistic sort, regarded taste as inevitably vitiated in proportion as it became public. Although Keats, again, was "certain of nothing but the holiness of the Heart's affections and the truth of the Imagination," he had little patience with Godwin's belief in "perfectibility" — "the nature of the world will not admit of it"; and the "Heart's affections" of which he speaks are as far removed from the temperamental "benevolism" of a John Gilbert Cooper as is the "reason" of Erasmus or Johnson from that of Charles Gildon. "I know nothing, I have read nothing," said the youthful Keats: ". . . there is but one way for me — the road lies through application, study, and thought." For

The difference of high Sensations with and without knowledge appears to me this — in the latter case we are falling continually ten thousand fathoms deep and being blown up again without wings and with all the horror of a bare shouldered creature — in the former case, our shoulders are fledge, and we go thro' the same air and space without fear.[8]

And following Reynolds — whose *Discourses* he greatly admired — Wordsworth dismissed any argument for taste which presupposes the validity of untutored sentiment: taste, he said, "can only be produced by severe thought and a long-continued intercourse with the best models of composition"; and the fundamental principles and intentions of such poets as Chaucer, Shakespeare, and Milton must be imbibed by any English poet or critic and woven into the texture of his mind. The poet, said Coleridge, must regulate himself "by principles, the ignorance or neglect of which would convict him of being no *poet*, but a silly or presumptuous usurper of the name" —

[8] Keats to J. H. Reynolds, May 3, 1818, *Letters* (ed. M. B. Forman, 1935), p. 140.

In a word by such a knowledge of the facts, material and spiritual, that most appertain to his art, as, if it have been governed and applied by *good sense*, and rendered instinctive by habit, becomes the representative and reward of our past conscious reasonings, insights, and conclusions, and acquires the name of TASTE.[9]

Indeed, "genius" is almost determined by the extent to which knowledge and experience are rendered intuitively and spontaneously applicable by strong conception and feeling. Shakespeare, said Hazlitt, possessed a knowledge "of the connecting links of the passions" which "anticipated and outdid all the efforts of the most refined art, not inspired and rendered instinctive by genius." "Talent," he added, "is a voluntary power, while genius is "involuntary." And the emphasis by British romantic critics on the "spontaneity" and "unconsciousness" of genius is by no means to be confused, as it occasionally has been, with an infinite capacity for not taking pains, and with the admittedly rather general desire in the nineteenth century to emancipate individual temperament. Shakespeare, said Coleridge, was "no mere child of nature": rather, he "studied patiently, meditated deeply, understood minutely, till knowledge, become habitual and intuitive, wedded itself to his habitual feelings, and at length gave birth to that stupendous power, by which he stands alone, with no equal or second in his class." [10] August von Schlegel contended that the Greeks were able to assume "a unison and proportion between all the faculties," whereas modern art and thought are aware of an "internal discord," and attempt to reconcile it by "hallowing the impressions of the senses, as it were, through a mysterious connection with higher feelings; while the soul, on the other hand, embodies its forebodings, or indescribable intuitions of infinity, in types and symbols borrowed from the visible world." [11] This "internal discord," and the struggle to reconcile it, were somewhat

[9] Coleridge, *Biographia Literaria* (1817; ed. Shawcross, 1907), II, 64.
[10] *Ibid.*, II, 19–20.
[11] Schlegel, *Lectures on Dramatic Art and Literature* (1809–1811), Lect. 1.

less pronounced in England. For "intuition" and the "impressions of the senses" had never been effectively separated there; and, as a consequence, it was not felt that sense-impressions particularly needed to be "hallowed" nor that intuitions, on the other hand, were completely "indescribable."

The intuitional assimilation of experience, and the capacity of feeling to capture interrelations, qualities, and significances, however elusive, and then to modify and render them organically and instantaneously pertinent, form the background of almost all the various conceptions of taste, genius, and imagination advanced in early-nineteenth-century English criticism and aesthetics; and had Hazlitt written his contemplated history of British philosophy, he would perhaps have sketched the rise and ramifications of this background with a revealing and certainly sympathetic insight. This conception of mind, which is very British both in looseness and in its joint empiricism and intuitionalism, was capable of many modifications which varied from a mildly skeptical relativism to a potential coöperation — such as Reynolds had earlier achieved — with many of the tenets of humanistic classicism. The extent of its flexibility and of its unusual capacity for eclecticism is peculiarly exemplified by Coleridge, who, as Mr. Wellek has well shown, was far from being the Kantian he is usually supposed to have been. A French writer has said that Mme Clotilde de Vaux, whom Comte regarded as his "inspiration," "never inspired Comte except with his own ideas"; and — certainly without implying any similarity in mental stature between Clotilde and Kant — we may say that Kant rarely inspired Coleridge except with his own ideas or with those which he had imbibed, as a youth, from the Christian Platonists.

v

By its loose and compromising empiricism, therefore, English romantic thought avoided both excessive relativism and mere emotionalism. Its major departure from classical precept and practice was in being somewhat naturalistic in its direction rather than frankly subjectivistic; for the intuitional empiricism upon which it relied was tempted to concentrate on the particular, and upon the revelation of its essential nature *as* a particular. This concentration had occasionally an almost scientific direction, as in Sir Charles Bell's *Lectures on the Anatomy and Philosophy of Expression* (1806), which took as their concern the natural expression of character in the face and figure of the human being, and the cause and control of this expression by the focusing of the various natural forces and relations which propel and animate the empirical universe. *King Lear*, said Hazlitt in a passage which evoked admiration from Keats, continually presents

the highest examples not only of the force of individual passion, but of its dramatic vicissitudes and striking effects arising from the different circumstances and characters of the persons speaking. We see the ebb and flow of the feeling, its pauses and feverish starts, its impatience of opposition, its accumulating force when it has time to recollect itself, the manner in which it avails itself of every passing word or gesture . . .[12]

The expression and character of the particular itself might thus become an objective goal for imaginative grasping; and beauty, accordingly, would be viewed as a sort of by-product which attends the fulfillment by a creature, object, or even an empirically rendered aesthetic form of its distinctive and individual function, significance, and nature. "Nothing seemed to escape him," said Joseph Severn, recalling his walks with Keats:

the motions of the wind — just how it took certain tall flowers . . . even the features and gestures of the passing tramps, the colour of one woman's hair, the smile on one child's face, the furtive animalism below the deceptive humanity in many of the vagrants, even the hats, clothes, shoes, wherever these conveyed the remotest hint as to the real self of the wearer.[13]

[12] Hazlitt, *Characters of Shakespear's Plays* (1817), in *Works* (ed. Howe, 1931–1934), IV, 259.
[13] William Sharp, *Life and Letters of Joseph Severn* (1892), p. 20.

It was the naturally "instinctive" and elusive character and meaning of the particular in which, for Keats, the poetical resided:

I go among the Fields and catch a glimpse of a Stoat or a fieldmouse peeping out of the withered grass — the creature hath a purpose and its eyes are bright with it. I go amongst the buildings of a city and I see a Man hurrying along — to what? the Creature has a purpose and his eyes are bright with it.

The "reasonings" of the human being are themselves a pursuit of "the same instinctive course as the veriest human animal you can think of," and possess a higher but fundamentally similar "grace":

May there not be superior beings amused with any graceful, though instinctive attitude my mind may fall into, as I am entertained with the alertness of a Stoat or the anxiety of a Deer? Though a quarrel in the Streets is a thing to be hated, the energies displayed in it are fine; the commonest Man shows a grace in his quarrel — By a superior being our reasonings may take the same tone — though erroneous they may be fine — This is the very thing in which consists poetry.[14]

Yet we may recall the striking evolution which took place in Keats two years before his premature death; and there is reason to believe that, had he lived even another twenty-five years longer, the course of both the poetry and the criticism of nineteenth-century England would have been somewhat different. "Some think," he later wrote, "I have lost that poetic ardor and fire 'tis said I once had." It gave him no regret; for "I hope," he continued, "I shall substitute a more thoughtful and quiet power." And even when he stated that the poetical is to be found in the distinctive function and "identity" of the particular alone, he was not really certain; for he added, "If so, [poetry] is not so fine a thing as philosophy — For the same reason that an eagle is not so fine a thing as a truth."

[14] To George and Georgiana Keats, Feb. 14 to May 3, 1819, *Letters*, pp. 316–317.

Indeed, it must not be forgotten that at least some awareness of the necessity of the universal is implied throughout most English romantic criticism. The object of poetry, said Wordsworth, "is truth, not individual and local, but general, and operative." Yet if English romantic criticism was cognizant of the universal, it tended to regard the universal as attainable only through the particular; it would have agreed, for example, with Sir Joshua Reynolds that Michelangelo's use of particularization was indispensable as a means of enlivening and enforcing the presentation of the ideal. "Nothing becomes real," said Keats, "till it is experienced"; "axioms in philosophy are not axioms until they are proved upon our pulses." And Hazlitt, who considered drama "the closest imitation of nature" because of its capacity to exhibit both the individual and the representative, felt that the concrete must serve as the starting point; if we know little of humanity, for example, "but its abstract and common properties, . . . we shall care just as little. . . . If we understand the texture and vital feeling, we can then fill up the outline, but we cannot supply the former from having the latter given." There seems also to have been an occasional hope, inferable if unformulated, of disclosing the naturalistic and almost independent "truth" or character of the particular and at the same time of revealing its participation or reflection of the ideal; and it is indicative of the compromising spirit of the English criticism of this period that it should have thus essayed to preserve this precarious and at bottom loosely empirical balance between the ideal and the concrete.

Perhaps the most successful attempt, certainly the most familiar, was that of Coleridge. Through a brilliant eclecticism, he tried to establish at least a theoretical mutual dependence between particular and universal by maintaining the vital ferment of potentiality inherent in the former and its organic transmutation into the latter. The particular, indeed, is not a separate and fixed totality at all: what appears as a finite and self-sufficient entity is only "a framework which the human imagination forms by its own limits, as the foot measures itself on the snow." Shakespeare, accordingly, did not merely abstract generalizations from his knowledge of specific individuals: rather, in addition to this secondary and merely assisting process, he grasped the living force, the law and active thread of connection, which binds the specific with the general; and it is characteristic that "in the Shakespearian drama there is a vitality which grows and evolves itself from within." It was the prerogative of Shakespeare

to have the *universal*, which is potential in each *particular*, opened out to him . . . not as an abstraction from observation of a variety of men, but as the substance capable of endless modifications, of which his own personal existence was but one, and to use *this one* as the eye that beheld the other, and as the tongue that could convey the discovery.[15]

Beaumont and Fletcher, for example, portray only "what could be put together and represented to the eye." Their piecemeal synthesis, that is, was a mere "abstraction" from the observation of various particulars, and lacks the germinating potentiality, the organic unfolding of process, which Shakespeare continually discloses. Their achievement is comparable to that of a man who

might put together a quarter of an orange, a quarter of an apple, and the like of a lemon and a pomegranate, and make it look like one round diverse coloured fruit. But nature, who works from within by evolution and assimilation according to a law, cannot do it. Nor could Shakespeare, for he too worked in the spirit of nature, by evolving the germ within by the imaginative power according to an idea.[16]

A power which can unite the relatively passive and empirical conception of the particular with the comprehension of the universal is necessarily an active one. "Taste," said Coleridge, therefore, must be "an intermediate faculty which connects the active with the passive powers of our nature, the intellect with the senses;

[15] Coleridge, Lecture vii (1818), *Miscellaneous Criticism* (ed. Raysor, 1936), p. 44.
[16] *Ibid.*, pp. 42–43.

and its appointed function is to elevate the *images* of the latter, while it realizes the *ideas* of the former." Coleridge's later assignment of this function to the imagination itself is characteristic of English romantic terminology. The later eighteenth century, in establishing and analyzing what constitutes taste, had so emphasized the active properties of the mind that the imagination gradually usurped the place which taste had been given. For "taste," as Wordsworth said, too often bears a popular connotation of a "passive" faculty or combination of faculties, whereas aesthetic insight is really impossible "without the exertion of a coöperating power in the mind of the Reader." Romantic criticism believed that it had found an appropriate term in "imagination"; for it wished to postulate a faculty which is at all times acutely aware, as "consequitive reasoning" is not, of the empirically concrete, and which is at the same time cognizant of all that reason, in its widest sense, can attain: a capacity, in other words, which, by drawing upon all facets of mind and feeling, conceives the particular as "adequate to an idea of reason," and effects an indissoluble "reconcilement," as Coleridge said, of "the general with the concrete; the idea with the image." Such an achievement is characterized by a "union of all that is essential in all the functions of our spirit," and by "an emotion tranquil from its very intensity"; and the imagination, since it connotes this comprehensive and energizing capacity, "is but another name," as Wordsworth stated, for "Reason in her most exalted mood."

VI

As it was resurrected during the eighteenth century, the conception of art as a unique and independent function or aspect of life was inevitably distinguished by a growing self-consciousness. Yet many of the figures of that century, including some who themselves advanced or indirectly aided this conception, seem to have felt that this self-consciousness, with its accompanying interest in aesthetic theory, was a symptom that Western art was moving into a more sophisticated and a less vital and gifted stage. Certainly, the general relativistic movement in Western European art is not without historical parallels which would possibly suggest as much. It is especially to be compared — as indeed it often has been — with the general tenor of classical art after the age of Pericles. The growing concern with the particularized character, which gathered impetus in sculpture and painting under the Alexandrian realists; the emphasis on "originality," which seems to have stemmed from the time of Alexander the Great and then to have augmented with the opening of the Christian era; the ultimate rejection of the mimetic theory of art by such theorists as Philostratus and the evoking of the creative imagination, "a wiser and subtler artist" — as Philostratus said — "than imitation": — such tendencies, of course, were merely surface indications of a growing self-consciousness in art, and of an increasing emphasis upon art as an independent exercise of the mind.

It has been well said that "The Greek knew not that he was an artist till his arts were well past their prime": his dominant conscious concern had been "Gods, heroes, and men" rather than art as such. The Greek use of art as a formative means to a further end is not to be confused, of course, with didacticism in the ordinary sense of the word. The assumption that art has little excuse for existence unless it discloses and inculcates the fundamental verities of life was therefore no more peculiar to Plato than it was unusually Philistine for Aristotle to state that "Children are to be instructed in painting . . . primarily because it makes them judges of the beauties of the human form." Mr. F. P. Chambers has justly contended that "If morality is an obstruction to the free creative impulses of Fine Art, — as modern aesthetics believe — under such obstruction did Fine Art in Greece begin her course; nor was she freed when she ran most strongly." And when Greece at length emancipated art: when it turned, that is, to the deliberate cultivation and study of art for itself, and to aesthetic theorizing, it discovered that its highest attainment in art was already in the past. Without pushing the parallel too far, or by any means collapsing into the ever-waiting arms of Spengler, we may admit that, like the pervasive philosophical shift which it mirrored, the great relativistic emancipation of art in the later eighteenth century at least brought with it a few of the problems which ancient art, as it acquired self-consciousness, had finally been forced to confront. The main problem with which European art was now faced was to find a centrality of purpose and direction. It may be questioned whether this centrality has really been found. Nor can criticism, from the onset of this epoch until the present day, be said to have furnished much lasting aid in the attempt to descry it, despite the isolated insights of its major spokesmen and the later addition of unparalleled technical means.

The manner in which leading English critics of the early nineteenth century avoided the excesses of both emotionalism and subjectivism is mainly attributable to a more than usually active presence in this period of qualities which are distinctively British: to the empirical but compromising good-sense which traditionally characterizes British thought at its happiest, and to a stubborn refusal to accept for long any systematization. Ways of thinking which have been customarily thought of as British have almost invariably shown a certain moderation as long as they have been confined to their homeland; and it is one of the interesting paradoxes of European history that, from the time of Duns Scotus, intellectual, as well as social, economic, and aesthetic tendencies, which have taken rise in Britain, have been carried to their logical conclusions elsewhere. We may agree, for example, with Engels, who, in praising England with faint damns, stated that "materialism is the natural-born son of Great Britain." Yet materialism in England, like so many other tendencies there, has largely preserved an amateur status; it remained for the later French Cartesians to systematize mechanism, and to conclude, by applying the rationalism of Descartes to the empiricism of Locke, that man is really a "machine." "In the eighteenth century," said Friedrich Schlegel

at its close, "the English were the first people of Europe, in literature, as in everything else. The whole of modern French philosophy was produced by that of Bacon, Locke, and other Englishmen. . . . Yet what a different appearance it assumed in France,
from that which it had always had in England!" The paradox of
English thought may be likened "to a man who bears every external mark of health and vigor, but who is by nature prone to a
dangerous distemper"; the distemper never became extreme enough
to "break out openly," and was therefore never "cured." Schlegel
seems almost to have surmised that the "materialistic disease" has
been mildly inherent in the English for so long that they themselves have become relatively immune to the epidemics with which
they periodically infect the continent. Utilitarianism, again, is un-
questionably the offspring of Britain. Yet few gifted English
thinkers were consistent in their utilitarianism; and the disparity
between the effeminate sociolatry of Comte and the liberal individualism of John Stuart Mill may serve as an exaggerated but
pertinent indication.

French critics often remind us, moreover, that the English are
traditionally "romantic." Some substantiation may perhaps be found
in the prevalent tenor of English literature as a whole. It is also
certainly true that many general tendencies which are thought of
as congenial to romanticism have been traditional with the English. One may note, for example, that Gothic architecture, long
after it had expired on the continent, survived in England well
into the seventeenth century. It even lingered on afterwards in
the provincial counties; and its eighteenth-century "revival" was
hardly so great a break with tradition as has occasionally been believed. British thought, moreover, which tends to prize immediacy and timeliness rather than abstraction and finality, has in all
periods exhorted "instincts" and "intuitions" which have a rather
emotional tinge. Yet it would be difficult to find a major British
figure who was comparable to Rousseau. The romantic "regener-
ation of literature in the eighteenth century," said Friedrich

Schlegel, "received its first impetus and its principal ruling direction from the poetry and the criticism of the English"; but he felt that German poetry and the earnest professionalism of German thought were required to develop its full romantic potentialities.

An enviable capacity to reconcile apparently inconsistent elements has been a familiar example of this moderation. We may recall the genuinely humanistic temper of many of Locke's sentiments. "The most singular phenomenon in the whole history of philosophy," said the puzzled Schlegel, "is perhaps the existence of such a man as Berkeley, who carried the attitudes of Locke so far as utterly to disbelieve the existence of the material world, and yet continued all the while a devout Christian bishop." Similarly, Hume, the prince of those that would live in the subjective, could retain and justify his neo-classic tastes, and associationism, under the Reverend John Gay, took rise within the tolerant confines of the Anglican church. This very moderation, with its resulting plasticity of mind, has permitted England to be the soil from which modern empirical relativism has stemmed and at the same time to remain a persistent seat of a broad, flexible, and unsystematized classical tradition. It may be questioned whether the strain of platonism which sometimes emerges in English thought is not more genuine, because more pliable and less methodized, than that on the continent; and there is also reason to believe that the spirit if not the letter of Christian humanism was perhaps more closely approached by a few Englishmen in the Renaissance than by its more ardent but less plastic exponents elsewhere. It is equally characteristic that the more representative figures of eighteenth-century England could reflect an almost Horatian sanity and good sense without degenerating into the bodiless and self-conscious urbanity typified by Voltaire; nor should one overlook the anomaly at this time of so authentic a Christian humanist as Dr. Johnson.

For British thought is especially the product of individuals rather than the collective architectural achievement of a movement or an age. "In speculation as in other things," Mr. Santayana has stated, "the Englishman trusts his inner man; his impulse is to soliloquize even in science." It is certainly true that although he may adopt from others — and occasionally with unparalleled sympathy and timeliness — elements which he deems "sensible" or which may seem to him to help explain his intuitions, the English thinker, from his suspicion of systems, has continually reverted to his own convictions as an individual, and reworked his philosophy afresh. The individual variety of British thought, which often transcends or disregards the general outlines of a movement or a period, is a consequence. But it also chances that, from the time of William of Occam, his convictions have usually been empirical; he is confident that experience both exists and teaches; and his watchword ultimately becomes the sensible remark of Edmund Burke — that "though no man can draw a stroke between the confines of day and night, yet darkness and light are upon the whole tolerably distinguishable." Hence the repetitive character of British thought — which also transcends the proclivities of an age — and its capacity to evoke despair in French logicians and bewilderment in German historians of philosophy. Indeed, English history as a whole, said Goethe, "repeats itself over and over again," and because it possesses so intrinsic a character, is "genuine, healthy, and therefore universal." Whether for better or worse, the history of British thought — like the British Constitution — almost deserves Johnson's description of Dryden's prose: it is "always another and the same."

The eighteenth-century transition in conceptions of art and taste is admittedly far-reaching in its implications. For if art is the interpreter of human values, aesthetic criticism, which must estimate the worth of this interpretation, is ultimately interwoven with man's entire thinking: it is interwoven with his ability to respond emotionally to rational ends, with his ethical premises and ideals, his religious aspirations, his various cosmologies, and the scientific abstractions he may choose to employ. Yet if this transition marks the general subsiding and interchange of certain very basic conceptions and values, it also witnessed the perseverance and readaptation of others. For, in varying degree, major figures of any age break through the shell of whatever concepts or premises of thinking that age may construct or generally accept. Moreover, through its traditional moderation, eclecticism, and repetitive self-scrutiny, the prevalent English thought of this transition retained a certain continuity both of procedure and, in some respects, of aim. It reworked and modified the empiricism and intuitionalism which it had inherited, and which had produced such troubled reverberations elsewhere. In doing so, it gradually evolved a loose but persistent body of aesthetic, moral, and psychological conceptions which underlay and even guided a notable flowering of literature. The pervasiveness of this body of assumptions renders it one of the few really effective means of linking together the English romantic poets and critics, while its elasticity is illustrated by the individuality, and even marked dissimilarity, which it permitted to these writers. But the unique fusion of its qualities gives it a broader and even perennial significance. For it is characteristically English, both in the varied adaptability which its looseness and lack of system permit and in its simultaneous continuity with British thought as a whole.

INDEX